TEACHING ONE CHILD:
A STRATEGY FOR DEVELOPING TEACHING EXCELLENCE

TEACHING ONE CHILD:

a strategy for developing teaching excellence

ERNEST SIEGEL, Ed.D.

Supervisor, Education of the Physically Handicapped
New York City Board of Education

EDUCATIONAL ACTIVITIES, INC.

Freeport, New York

Library of Congress Catalogue Card Number: 72-92411

Printed In The United States of America

For her critical review of the entire manuscript, for her wisdom, for her patience with me during the numerous sojourns to my study, and for her confidence in me, I gladly dedicate this book

to Rita ——

my wife

my colleague

my love.

Acknowledgments

Many individuals have supported, encouraged, and assisted me in the completion of this book. To all of them, I express my genuine appreciation:

To Frank Gisonti, Professor of Education, Queens College, New York; Gerald Posnack, teacher of homebound, New York City Board of Education; and Allan Schulps, Special Education Coordinator at the Center for Multiple-Handicapped Children, New York City Board of Education for their genuine interest in this project from its inception. These colleagues are talented practitioners and I have utilized many of their ideas.

To those educators who either reviewed or discussed portions of the manuscript thereby enabling me to crystallize my own thoughts. These include James Everett, Professor of Special Education, University of New Mexico; Ben Brooks, Director of Special Education, Appalachian State University; John McLeod, Director of Institute of Child Guidance and Development, University of Saskatchewan; Louis Bransford, Director of Utilization and Services, Federation of Rocky Mountain States; and Leon Schuchman, Supervisor, Bureau for Education of the Physically Handicapped, New York City Board of Education.

To the students of my various college courses for sharing their knowledge, experiences, and critical opinions with me.

To Helen Lorick, my first supervisor of home instruction. Her love for and understanding of children, her high regard and standards for teachers, and her intense awareness of the unique value of the one-to-one setting in nurturing pedagogical expertise must surely have planted the seeds for this project.

And finally, I am grateful to my sister, Rebecca Holtzman (a free lance author) and proud of my son, Paul (a talented eighteen year old college junior) for typing and editing portions of the original manuscript.

Ernest Siegel

Preface

Teaching One Child: A strategy for developing teaching excellence will remain with us because it says something that hasn't been said quite this way before; and, the book is important because it needed to be said. In the tradition of Jean-Marc-Gaspard Itard, Anne Sullivan, and that neglected army of great teachers, Ernest Siegel has written a book on that most pristine yet exciting setting —the one teacher-one child culture. With love, with respect for people and for learning, his wisdom illustrates the Latin origin of the word "educate." Truly, Dr. Siegel shares with us here ways and possibilities for bringing out, eliciting, and developing responses and capabilities from those who would learn with him. For, in the profound sense, this book is not merely to guide the child's learning—although that would have been enough—but, as fundamentally, the teacher's learning. In the profound sense, the book demonstrates that the significant teaching-learning interaction does not polarize teacher and learner but is a time for each to engage in giving of oneself and garnering the prizes of enlightenment and understanding.

What are the most appropriate "descriptors" of Dr. Siegel? Special educator, humanitarian, clinician, but most of all, teacher. And this book? Individually prescribed instruction, individualized instruction, but, foremost, individual instruction. Then, what is there to be learned?

That, as exemplified in the lives of Itard's Wild Boy, Helen Keller, May Seagoe's Paul, and Dr. Siegel's pupil's, Man's capabilities are educable,

That there are classes of individuals while, essentially, individuals in classes learn alone,

That the difference between diagnostic and normative teaching is the difference between inductive and deductive procedures, process and no-process, creating and duplicating,

That learning must be counted in ideational and inspirational hours, not in clock hours,

That the process of teaching requires a deep interest in people and an interest in learning for the sake of learning; all the rest is commentary.

That, as with "one-on-one" in basketball, a "one-and-one" learning relationship teaches about such human matters as timing, tempo changes, tactics, and strategies,

That children know best about what they get, and what they want, and what they need,

And, the prepotent lesson, that individual learning is the building block for group learning—both for child and teacher, if for no other reason than that the "one-and-one" interaction guarantees feedback.

There is profit to be earned in picking apart this book, and as much for purposes of comprehending oneself as the work.

Burton Blatt, Centennial Professor
Director, Division of Special
Education and Rehabilitation
Syracuse University

Contents

NOTE: Throughout this book the child, the teacher, and the school principal are referred to as "he"; the supervisor of tutoring programs and the practicum instructor are referred to as "she"; the parent emphasized is the mother. All of this is arbitrary but it would have been awkward to say continuously "he or she" and "his or her." The reader of course is free to substitute the sex of his or her choice.

Foreword

September, 1951. That's when it all started. I began teaching homebound children—children who were too handicapped physically or emotionally to attend school and who had to receive their instruction at home. My previous experience consisted of student-teaching and then teaching in regular public school classes, but now I would be working with one child at a time.

In the early part of my career as a teacher of home instruction, I made a most remarkable discovery. Looking back now, I am sure that it must have come about gradually. Based upon the feedback data from having taught and observed my "class" of individuals and from discussions with some of my colleagues, an idea germinated, then grew almost imperceptibly, but the total impact was one of sudden realization: Given a child who *can* learn (that is, one whose physical or intellectual limitations are not so grave as to interfere with learning) and who *wants* to learn (that is, a child who is emotionally "tuned in" to learning), he can often progress faster with three to six weekly hours of individual instruction than he would in the customary thirty hour school week!

This discovery concerning the child had its counterpart discovery concerning the teacher. It can best be put in the form of a question: If the process of individual instruction can effect such dramatic gains in the child as a learner, might it not respectively promote similar growth in the teaching skills of his instructor? Little by little, I became aware that many of my home instruction colleagues seemed several notches above the "norm" in instructional expertise. Certainly, I (in an objective way, I hope) was beginning to sense a feeling of pedagogic competence different from any which I had ever experienced when teaching groups of children. Years later, in my role of college instructor, I continued investigating this hypothesis by asking my students: "Among those of you who have taught in both settings—one child at a time as well as in groups—do you think the experience of teaching individual children helped you become more proficient in the classroom?" The answer was invariably in the affirmative—and enthusiastically so!

Recently, American education has come under grave criticism. The charges range from some social activists' "educational genocide" to Charles E. Silberman's (CRISIS IN THE CLASSROOM) ". . . mutilation of spontaneity, of joy of learning, of pleasure of creating, of joy of self. . . ." In actuality, it may very well be that central to most of the ills of the institution of education is simply the lack of a precise understanding regarding the teaching-learning process. After all, if a child isn't taught properly, he suffers not only educationally, but psychologically, socially, vocationally, and economically as well. Similarly, the teacher who is not teaching effectively can very likely develop negative attitudes towards the child since he is the symbol of the teacher's failure.

The major thrust of this book is that experience in teaching one child at a time—being preparatory to teaching groups of children—is the key to teaching excellence. So, if you are:

an instructor of education courses, create the logistics whereby the teacher trainees can derive guided, ongoing experience teaching one child at a time as well as the traditional group student-teaching.

a school administrator, utilize supervised tutoring as a prime ingredient of in-service training for the inexperienced or below average teacher.

a student-teacher, suggest to the college supervisor and to the cooperating teacher that some individual instruction be incorporated into your student-teaching program. Ask them to provide guidance and supervision (observe, make suggestions, demonstrate, evaluate) to you during this experience so that you will garner optimal benefits from this phase of your training.

a teacher, get experience in teaching one child at a time. Speak to your practicum instructor or to your principal about it. Teach a neighbor's child, a relative's child, a colleague's child, even your own child. Volunteer (anti-poverty programs, church or civic organizations, parent-sponsored organizations such as United Cerebral Palsy, Association for Children with Learning Disabilities, Associations for Help of Retarded children, etc.) or "moonlight" (e.g., summer camp programs, private reading clinics, commercial tutoring centers, private tutoring on a fee basis). The rewards can be invaluable.

a paraprofessional, cherish the tutoring experience which your present position may afford you; it will stand you in good stead should you later decide upon teaching as a career.

Ernest Siegel

Chapter I

Introduction

Background

The word "education" will generally evoke a mental image of a classroom in a school building, a teacher and a room full of pupils. In other words, teaching and learning have become synonymous with *group* education. Upon reflection, however, one realizes that it has not historically always been thus. Didn't Biblical man educate his son in a one-to-one relationship? Wasn't the apprentice-journeyman format essentially a one teacher–one pupil educational system? Aristotle was taught—and in turn taught others—on an individual basis. Anne Sullivan taught Helen Keller, Itard instructed and trained the Wild Boy of Aveyron and, in literature, Professor Higgins coached and polished Eliza Doolittle—all using the one teacher-one pupil instructional setting. The Oxford scholar was educated similarly. Even today, one of the philosophical tenets of Special Education (education which meets the needs of atypical children) is that instruction should be individualized—small classes, modification of approaches, content area geared to the child's interests, etc. Indeed, under certain circumstances (for instance, students in hospitals and homebound pupils), children receive their formal "classroom" education entirely on a one-to-one ratio. The recognition of the merits of individualization does not confine itself solely to those in Special Education. General educators (that is, those professionals concerned with the problems and practices in the education of normal children) agree that an ideal educational climate is one which takes into account the concept that each child is an individual. In fact, our current anti-poverty programs, in stressing the tutorial aspect of education, recognize the merits of one-to-one teaching.

Individualized Instruction

The concept of individualized instruction is one that has been ingrained in the educational philosophy of a democratic society, largely reflecting our awareness of the "whole" child, our recognition of the uniqueness of the individual vis-à-vis his distinctive personality, attitude, values, style, needs, etc., and our concern—especially currently—with individual rights. A great deal has been written about individualized instruction; in fact, our interest in this topic can be seen by the recent formation of organizations, both regionally and nationally, devoted entirely to the furthering of individualized instruction. Some examples of individualized instructional programs are:

Team teaching. This is an organizational concept in which the several teachers involved function as specialists rather than as generalists. They work cooperatively, each assuming a given subject area responsibility, often spreading vertically among several grades. Individualization is fostered because:

1. each teacher possesses (or develops) in-depth specialty strengths and can thus present more of a selection from this greater range;
2. flexible programming is possible since the child's education is no longer dependent upon his experiences with only a single teacher;
3. there is greater pupil mobility vertically; and
4. cooperative planning in curriculum design, evaluation,

and instruction focuses upon the needs of the individual child.

Non-Graded classes. In these classes, the traditional grouping of children by age and grade is abolished. What ensues is greater heterogeneity in background, ages, abilities, and interests. This increased diversification permits—indeed, demands—considerable flexibility in curriculum, programming, and grouping within a given classroom. Dawson (1962, 28) feels that non-graded classes:

1. take into account the unevenness of development and growth.
2. stress individual differences in setting up instructional goals.
3. eliminate anxiety caused by fear of "formal failure" on report cards or at promotion time.
4. challenge *all* the students—". . . the bright to work at a higher level, the average to strive for continuous progress, and the slow learner or late bloomer to keep trying."

Differentiated staffing. This plan enables some of the teaching staff to devote all of their time and energies to pupil guidance, and developing individualized curricula rather than to instruction. Other teachers develop and teach their own subject area specialty under this system. Many of the non-teaching tasks are performed by paraprofessionals and volunteers, thereby permitting the instructors to provide further individualized attention.

Contract plan. Under this system, the child meets infrequently with his teacher. The traditional concepts of the school day and periods of instruction are abolished. The child receives his "contract," goes over it with his teacher, and is then largely on his own, as he proceeds to fulfill the contract. Thus, the child is encouraged to engage in independent research and study. He may go to libraries, lectures, and museums; sit in on some classrooms for background material; and must meet with his teacher periodically to discuss his project in its various stages.

Open Classroom. This system was pioneered in England and is often referred to as the "Infant School," "English Primary School," or "Open Corridor." Some of its major features (Silberman, 221-235) are:

1. Stationary desks and chairs are not used. Interest areas (e.g., Reading corners, Arithmetic corners, Music areas, a playhouse) are set up.

2. The children work in small groups or individually. The teacher circulates among the groups; on the few occasions when she wishes to instruct the entire class, the children gather around her, some sitting on chairs, others on the floor.

3. The children are not physically confined to the classroom, but spill over into the closets, halls, lobbies, corridors, playground, etc.

4. Silence is not generally in order. The children talk constantly but purposefully to one another, to the teacher, to classroom visitors, to *themselves!*

5. There is a richness of materials: e.g., a table on which are jars of vanilla, coffee, flowers, etc., and a sign inviting the children to smell these different substances; a water table where youngsters are free to drop various objects into containers of water to see their splash and to observe whether or not they will float.

6. A great deal of administrative flexibility prevails: a child in the throes of a temporary stressful situation may be permitted to attend school only part of the day; another immature, overly dependent child's mother is, in the beginning, invited to attend school with him; staggered ad-

mission may be set up to give the teacher the opportunity to become better acquinted with the class; flexible hours of attendance accommodate working parents—some children arriving as early as 7 A. M.

7. There is considerable self-discipline and self-direction.

The rationale for this system is that it takes into account the imprecise correspondence of developmental age to chronological age and matches the methods and materials with each child's unique developmental profile. It encourages the child who is young—and therefore relatively non-verbal—to learn by doing and discovering rather than by teacher verbalism. It enables the child to "play" manipulatively with concrete, physical materials and socially with his peers. Finally, it makes it possible for the teacher to guide the child's progress from random activity to more structured experiences, to judge when to let the child alone and when to intervene (i.e., teach) and, in short, to "capitalize" upon the occasion (Silberman, 213-221).

There are, of course, pitfalls in this approach. Hechinger (1971, 11) warns that any adaptation of this system by the American public schools be done *gradually* (that is how it evolved in England). Permissiveness should not become an end in itself, substituting for substance. Structure—albeit, subtle—is indeed needed since children "doing their own thing" aimlessly will result in destructiveness and in children disturbing one another (instead of benefiting from each other's presence). He further states that in England this system was developed by the local classroom teacher and was not mandated by curriculum experts and outside specialists.

Individually prescribed instruction. (IPI) Under this plan, the child proceeds from objective to objective as he completes his individual "prescription" which has been carefully prepared for him by the teacher. For the most part, the children work individually, at their own pace, and at their own level—which may vary even in the different subject areas. Although each child belongs to a class and a classroom, there is considerable movement as he leaves his room to proceed to a particular materials center in order to complete his prescription. The teachers engage in very little group instruction or lecturing, but spend most of their time observing, diagnosing, and prescribing for the individual child.

Work-study programs. These are programs for the slow learner, non-motivated, potential school dropout, or the delinquent. They are established in recognition of the high probability that these pupils will enter the field of work instead of seeking further education. Their individual needs—ego-building, job preparatory skills and attitudes, and motivation to study—are met by assigning them to a part-time job (for remuneration) while they attend classes for part of the day.

The classroom experiences dovetail with the work portion of the program, not only in the logistics of scheduled time-slots, but in syllabus as well. In other words, the instructors, being aware of the individual pupil's job, gear the course content to his ongoing work experiences. The two aspects of the program, instead of functioning independently (possibly at cross-purposes), mesh, thereby increasing the individual's incentive to study and simultaneously fostering greater work skills.

(In the interest of clarity, it should be pointed out that the same term, "work-study" is used to denote federally subsidized programs which assist needy college students by providing them with part-time job opportunities, usually at the college itself—e.g., librarian assistants. Here, however, the student is "on his own": The job's only purpose is to make it financially possible for the student to enroll and to remain in college; in no way do the college courses center around the job.)

Resource room. This is a vehicle which enables an "exceptional" child, (one with a learning, behavioral, and/or health problem) to remain in a regular classroom instead of being placed in a special class for the handicapped. The regular classroom teacher notes the child's problems and makes the referral to the resource room teacher. There, a specially trained teacher diagnoses the child's educational problems, evaluates the degree of severity, and devises a prescription. The child attends the resource room part of the day and his regular class for the remainder. This can go on for a full term or for part of it.

The resource room teacher offers corrective instruction, consulting with the regular classroom teacher concerning the implementation of the prescription in the regular classroom, and may, upon receiving the referral, make one or several classroom observations to determine for himself the kind and the extent of the problem. Before discharging the child from the resource room, the resource teacher may, in addition to consulting with the regular teacher, make further classroom observations to ascertain whether or not his suggestions are helping the classroom teacher. He may even demonstrate some of the prescribed measures to the classroom teacher.

Crisis teacher. In a sense, this alternative is an extension of the resource room teacher concept, except that it entails only children with emotional disturbance. Morse (1966, 252) believes that the crisis teacher must be talented in remedial reading, must have a thorough knowledge of curriculum, and should be skilled in life-space interviewing (a method of talking to a child in such a way that his feelings become clear to the interviewer; it can also be done for disciplinary purposes). In addition to the roles usually associated with any teacher, the crisis teacher may, at times, have to talk "man to man" to the child, become a surrogate parent, or serve as a counselor. Thus, the possible range of courses of action taken by the crisis teacher is necessarily broad, in deference to the broad spectrum of possible problems inherent in the "whole child": The activity could be tutoring. On the other hand, a diversionary activity may be needed. At times, an intensive life-space session is warranted; yet, in other instances, an informal talk will do. Morse (253) sums up: "In short, what is done is what any teacher would want to do were it possible to determine action by the needs of the child rather than the large group learning process in a classroom. . . ."

Enrichment within the regular classroom. There are three broad plans for accommodating the gifted in the public schools: ability grouping or "segregation", acceleration or "skipping", and enrichment within the regular class. Passow (1960, 31) points out that the third is the most widely adopted plan, particularly in the elementary school. The principal reason for its popularity is that flexible programming which can stimulate and challenge the gifted child intellectually is possible within the regular class—a setting which provides much-needed interpersonal experiences with his social peers.

Of course, the concept of enrichment holds considerable validity in the education of all children, not just the gifted. We seek to enrich—instead of "water down"—the curriculum of the slow learner; optimal educational experiences for the disadvantaged require enrichment in the interests of fostering motivation and relevancy; and negativism, hostility, withdrawal, and apathy among some emotionally disturbed are dealt with through an enriched environment. The process of individualization of instruction is completely interwoven with the principle of enrichment since the latter involves capturing the attention of, catering to the interests and needs of, and providing broader based, richer, and more meaningful experiences for the individual pupil.

Interclass ability grouping. This is probably the most common method of achieving individualization in classrooms throughout the nation. It involves dividing the class into groups (based on ability) for some subject areas—primarily Reading, and often Arithmetic. The number of groups vary; two and three are the usual number of groups, though an ingenious teacher may occasionally set up four. The teacher works actively with one group, while the others do directed, independent work (e.g., specific silent reading assignments, written work, etc.). The teacher, before leaving the group he is actively instructing and going on to the next group, assigns these children independent work and ascertains that they understand directions. Optional work (such as "free reading", starting homework, etc.) is provided to take into account children who finish their assigned independent work early. At no time is non-goal directed "busy" work, per se, necessary. Instead, all of the assignments and activities are unified, the teacher having made definite plans for all children in all groups to be occupied purposefully throughout the lesson. Despite this division into groups, the feeling of belonging to the class as a whole is nourished by bringing all groups together at the lesson's end for a brief period of sharing, recounting, and summarizing. Teaching in this way requires that the instructor be highly organized and that he plan fully for all pupils.

Unit method of instruction. Like inter-class ability grouping, this method has been used for decades by many teachers. It was promoted by the "learning by doing" philosophy and is synonomous in many ways with the concept of the "activities program". It consists of teaching by units of study rather than by the traditional division into subject matter areas. The topic of concern usually focuses upon some aspect of the curriculum. In Social Studies, for instance, "How the South Grew and Changed," "Recreation in the United States", "Man's Efforts to Achieve Peace," "Our Water Supply," "Our Northern Neighbors," "How Man Travels—Yesterday and Today," "Contributions of the American Negro," etc.

The teacher launches the unit (providing motivation), oversees it, acts as advisor to the various committees and brings them all together in a culmination activity—e.g., an assembly program, a trip, making a summary tape recording and/or film, a special class newspaper, even a test. Throughout the unit, the various subject areas are intergrated. Thus, a Social Studies topic may very often utilize Math, Science, Art, Music, etc. Remedial work and drill can be provided functionally.

The class works in committees, each responsible for a particular part of the overall topic. Within each committee, individual children will have different responsibilities.

The children prepare their individual contributions by visiting libraries and museums, taking trips, consulting with experts, conducting interviews, writing letters requesting information, etc. They often meet (voluntarily) after school at a committee member's home to continue their work on the unit.

The pupils select their own committees and make decisions regarding individual responsibilities, target dates, modes and lengths of presentations, means of obtaining information, etc. Thus, individualization is insured in many ways: the child works in small groups, at his own pace, in his individual style, in his area of interest, making his own decisions; also, he can be helped by the teacher individually during classroom committee work time.

• • •

Further examples of individualized instruction can be found in the Montessori Schools which capitalize upon the innate desire of children for work, predictability, and structure while stressing their individuality in terms of ability, level of accomplishment, motivational source, and sensory modality style. Most private schools further foster individualization of instruction by reducing class size, employing teacher aides, utilizing a variety of materials, working closely with parents, and by providing auxiliary services such as speech therapy and guidance.

Special Education, of course, abounds with examples of individualized instruction. Smaller class size, specially trained teachers, modified curriculum, special methods and materials, readily available diagnostic information about each pupil—all promote individualization. Additional factors are the employment of teacher aides, the assignment of a third ("floating") teacher between two special classes, the utilizing of an itinerant teacher and other consultants in such areas as visual training, corrective communication skills, and body image development, and provisions for such auxiliary services as psychotherapy, physiotherapy, and occupational therapy. In addition, private schools' as well as public schools' special classes often work cooperatively with the parent, thereby meeting the individual needs of the child more fully.

Individual Instruction

There is a difference between *individualized* instruction and *individual* instruction. In a sense, the one child-one teacher setting can be subsumed under the generic definition of "individualized instruction." In many ways, however, individual instruction should be regarded as the epitome of individualized instruction: There are tremendous advantages which accrue to both teacher and pupil only during sustained one-to-one instruction.

The reader should understand that this book patently avoids creating an issue rooted in the dichotomy of tutoring vs. classroom instruction. The following quotation from p. 45 sets the tone and enables the reader to sense this work's tenets and to view its perspectives:

> It should be made abundantly clear that as each of these advantages is presented, a case is not being developed for all

teachers to teach only individually; this would not be feasible, nor even desirable from any standpoint—financially, administratively, educationally. One group of teachers is not being pitted against another. What is being advocated is for *all* teachers to receive *some* one-to-one teaching experiences, and that this will make them more proficient in the classroom.

Likewise, it is advocated that *some* children will benefit from individual tutoring *some* times. This tutoring can occur either in the classroom or outside of it, as part of the school day or after school hours. Only under compelling circumstances—severe physical or emotional handicap—should the child be educated by tutoring alone and denied the social experiences inherent in classroom instruction.

The prime reason for insisting that a child learn in a group setting, wherever possible, is the opportunity for socialization. Additional benefits include group stimulation, motivation through competitiveness opportunity to observe "normal" points of references regarding standards of behavior and performance, and enhanced emotional security stemming from the feeling of belonging, of being part of the group, and of being "normal."

Despite the merits of and the philosophy (legal as well as administrative) favoring group instruction, there will always be those who need individual instruction, whether to the exclusion of, or in conjunction with the regular class program. The advantages of one-to-one instruction for the child are well-known. Some of them are:

1. The lesson can be "tailor-made".

2. The teacher can observe the child more closely and "know" him more fully.

3. Instant evaluation is often possible.

4. A child's inconsistent style can be more easily accommodated. The low phase of his cycle—e.g., poorer than usual performance, daydreaming, depressed or hostile moods, lack of motivation—can be dealt with more effectively. Conversely, the tutor is in a unique position to recognize the child's high phase and to take his "flame and fan it."
5. Distractibility can be reduced.
6. Greater flexibility can ensue.
7. More continuity of instruction is possible.
8. In many instances, the teacher can work closely with the parent.
9. The child who is self-conscious in the presence of a classroom of children may be less so in the company of one teacher only.
10. The one-to-one relationship can be ego-building. After all, the tutor is there only for him, thus demonstrating the child's worth.
11. Tutoring can be therapeutic and serve as an instrument of intervention, often reversing the direction of a negative spiral in performance and/or behavior.

It is often said that the best way to learn to teach is by teaching! But there is a vast difference between teaching small groups of children (individualized instruction) and teaching one child (individual instruction). Even in those instances in which the teacher attempts to tutor a single child in the midst of a classroom of other children, there are still many factors which will militate against the development of optimal pedagogical skills: the periods of one-to-one instruction are too short, there are too many distracting elements, there frequently is no opportunity to complete the individual child's lesson, and the responsibility towards the other children drastically diminishes the teacher's sense of priority and continuity regarding the individual child. These factors are virtually non-existent in instructional settings in which the teacher can devote his *full* attention to the individual child.

In fact, this book is dedicated to the proposition that the opportunity to teach one child at a time on an in-depth, unhurried, ongoing, systematic basis is the single most important ingredient in nurturing teaching excellence. **ALL TEACHERS, THEREFORE, SHOULD ACQUIRE CONSIDERABLE GUIDED EXPERIENCE IN ONE-TO-ONE TEACHING PREFERABLY DURING THEIR PRE-SERVICE TRAINING—OR IF NOT THEN, FINALLY DURING IN-SERVICE TRAINING.**

It is probably no accident that so many of those educators who have made monumental contributions to education—special as well as regular—have had backgrounds in fields which entail considerable experience with one child at a time: Psychology—Piaget, Gillingham, Skinner, Bruner, Kirk, Dunn, Cruickshank, Frostig, Kephart, Lehtinen, Bannatyne, Clements, Fernald. Medicine (including psychiatry)—Montessori, Gesell, Orton, Strauss, Birch, Bender. Speech and Hearing—Myklebust, Johnson, Wepman, Barry, McGinnis, Fitzgerald, DeHirsh. Optometry—Getman, Solan. Occupational Therapy—Ayres.

There is a major trend in education towards including tutoring (i.e., one teacher–one child setting) as part of a child's total instructional experiences. You can hardly pick up an educational journal, article, or for that matter, even a newspaper without finding some reference to a new tutoring program. The emphasis on individualization of instruction as a humanizing force and the concept of compensatory education have given impetus to the demands for such programs. Moreover, the availability of federal funds—for research as well as for service—has made it possible to implement tutoring projects at an unprecedented accelerated pace.

There are many current tutoring programs, in special as well as in general education. Some examples follow:

Home instruction. If a child is so ill physically or emotionally that he can not attend school, many communities will send teachers into the home. (Mental retardation is not usually a criterion for admission to home instruction since school systems often have special classes for children who are "only" mentally retarded. Of course, there is overlap, and the same child who is physically or emotionally handicapped may also be mentally retarded, in which case, home instruction can be provided.) In some rural or suburban localities home instruction will begin after the teaching day by the regular classroom teacher. In large cities, specially trained and licensed teachers of the homebound are provided. Each teacher is responsible for a wide age and grade range, for a variety of subjects, and has been trained in the nature and needs of various kinds of handicapped. The instruction periods are approximately an hour to an hour and a half in length, and the weekly number of periods range from several days to five days. The homebound child's education can be augmented with such technological aids as educational TV, special radio programs, home-to-school telephone, teleclass, etc.

"Teacher-Mom" program. The pupil population is composed of those children who are excluded from the classroom because of profound behavior disorders: neuroses, psychoses (including schizophrenia), autism, brain damage, etc. The severity of their impairment would ordinarily mean that these children, in their current state, stay at home (with or without instruction) or perhaps even be committed to an institution. The point is that they are simply not ready to engage in group situations. The "teacher-mom" program's philosophy is that these children are better served if they can remain home but leave it daily to attend some school—even with nominal peer contact. The teachers are made up of volunteers who are selected on the basis of their own ad-

justment, warmth, and projected ability to empathize with their handicapped pupils. They teach one child at a time and are under the supervision of a trained Special Education teacher. The school building is usually one which also has been "volunteered", for example, a church. A number of children, say ten, will each be instructed individually in a separate room by the "teacher-mom" for two hours daily. The supervising teacher goes from room to room observing, diagnosing the teaching-learning process, encouraging, suggesting, demonstrating. There is an initial orientation period for the "teacher-moms" followed by in-service training. A child is assigned two "teacher-moms", each teaching him on two different days of the week. The remaining school day, the one in which the children receive no instruction, is used as an in-service training day for all the "teacher-moms". A staff of consulting specialists (psychologists, psychiatrists, speech therapists, etc.) are available. Special materials in a professional library are often housed in the supervising teacher's office and hence, are easily accessible to the staff.

George T. Donahue and Sol Nichtern pioneered this approach and authored *Teaching the Troubled Child* (New York, the Free Press, 1965), the definitive book in this field, describing in detail and evaluating the results of the first major program, the Elmont Program. Needless to say, this program is controversial. Fenichel (1966) in a quaintly titled article, "MAMA or M.A.?" opposes the one-to-one setting as the *only* alternative, criticizes the program for having excluded the child's parents from the team, and, above all, feels that the education of these children with special needs requires specially trained teachers instead of untrained volunteers.

Hospital Instruction. Hospitalized children receive their instruction individually or, at times, in small groups. Like the homebound teacher, the hospital teacher must develop proficiency in teaching a wide range of levels and subjects, since he generally encounters a wide age range of hospitalized pupils. The teacher must be extremely flexible in deference to such variables as long and short stays, ambulatory and non-ambulatory cases, different levels of intelligence, diverse backgrounds, etc. The matter of logistics is a vital one as the teacher must seek to dovetail the instructional program with other hospital services needed by the child.

Educational Therapy. The line of demarcation between individual instruction and therapy, though a valid one from the standpoint of professional training and background, methodology, emphasis, and even semantics, is not an impervious one. In fact, the dual roles—teacher and therapist—meet in the role of the "educational therapist". However, even for the multitude of teachers who have undergone the standard teacher training—i.e., trained to *teach,* not *treat*—it is hoped that their total impact upon the pupils is therapeutic (for those children who need this) as well as educational. Goldberg (1952) showed that tutoring had a therapeutic effect among schizophrenic children displaying reading disabilities. Similarly, Donahue and Nichtern (1965, 5) believe that "fear and anxiety, insecurity, hyperactivity, intrinsic personality distortions strongly suggested the need for a one-to-one emphatic teaching relationship" and that "children who are unpredictable and subject to extreme mood swings would need the total flexibility in programming inherent in one-to-one teaching." Connor (1964, 29) views the tutorial relationship in home instruction as "an almost unlimited chance for multifaceted personal development", pointing out that "here is an unthreatening situation for frank identification and recognition of the level of function, acceptance of recognized immediate and long-range goals, and an appreciation of minute accomplishments." Aronov (1970, 76) considers the tutorial process an ideal setting for providing success-assured activities, so necessary for many of the learning disabled children. A by-product of a tutoring program, in which volunteer women tutored dyslexic public school pupils, was the improved behavior of the children. (Jones, 1969, 536).

Therapeutic elements, then, can exist simply by virtue of being tutored, even by a non-therapist: a high degree of structure and predictability, the "tailor-made" curriculum fostering success, the gradual, systematic, development of responsibility and initiative, the enhanced self-concept resulting from being the recipient of the tutor's *individual* attention and concern, the anxiety reduction associated with sharing time with just the teacher as opposed to having to "make it" in front of the whole class, etc. In addition to these, there are important therapeutic ingredients which are possible only when an educational therapist (who is often a psychologist by training and believes in treating the child via the instructional process) is the teacher: the therapist's "know-how" regarding the nurturing and interpretations of the child's projections; his ability to utilize such techniques as play therapy; his skill in evaluating the child-parent relationship clinically and his ability to counsel the parent when necessary; his knowledge of how to use educational goals to help develop reality boundaries and to make the child aware of his own role in effecting events. Finally, the therapist-patient relationship is a very special one and is vital in effecting optimal adjustment for many emotionally handicapped.

The Itinerant Teacher. The itinerant teacher program is another means of meeting a child's tutoring needs without necessitating his transfering out of his regularly assigned classroom. The itinerant teacher, specially trained, travels from school to school, performing two basic functions:

1. advising the regular classroom teacher of special methods, techniques, and modifications which can help him in remediating a child's disabling educational problems

2. providing the child with individual instruction.

On the day that the itinerant teacher visits the school, designated children from various classrooms leave their regular class and meet with him for individual lessons—either singly or in small groups. One itinerant teacher may be a specialist in the Speech and Hearing field, offering corrective speech training. Another may be trained to work with blind pupils, teaching them Braille and counseling them in general study skills (e.g., note-taking). Some itinerant teachers specialize in remedial reading. Some school systems have recently established an itinerant teaching program for the minimally brain-injured (or the "learning disabled"). These children are enrolled in a regular classroom but can now receive periodic tutoring from the itinerant teacher in such areas as perceptual training, listening skills, study habits, etc.

Tutoring programs in public school classes. There are many examples of tutoring occurring in public school classes. The presence of volunteers, teacher aides, or student teachers can make classroom tutoring possible either by the teacher or by the assistant. Technological advents such as the teaching machine, programmed instruction materials, the "talking typewriter" (formally know as the Responsive Environment Program) make it possible for children to work independently for periods of time. In this way, the classroom teacher is freed to spend some of his time working with one child individually.

Children from higher classes can tutor younger children part of the day. The "buddy" system of studying has been going on for years: at a given time and for a specific purpose, a child is assigned a classmate as a "buddy"; they engage in some activity such as studying spelling. "Classroom Pairing," a system developed by Orlick and Ruchlis (n.d.) works on the principle that since any primary class has a wide range of abilities, there will necessarily be some pupils who need tutoring, and others who will be able to tutor. The class is thus divided into pairs—a tutor and a tutee.

(This differs from the "buddy" system in that the pairing here is based on matching the need of one child with the ability of another; the "buddy" system simply pairs up "neighboring" children.) Quite a few schools are experimenting with non-graded classes similar to the old "one-room schoolhouse" concept. In this environment, the younger pupils are often tutored by their older classmates.

If a class is small enough, a teacher may find the time to teach several children, one-at-a-time, while the remainder of the class is working independently. Many teachers find that this is possible to accomplish, discrediting the myth that each child in a class of thirty children requires one-thirtieth of the teacher's time.

Tutoring programs augmenting public school classes. Many tutoring programs take place outside of the school after school hours. A child may receive private tutoring in his own home or in the tutor's office. The range of the subject matter goals is vast, stretching from a six-year old child needing additional help in beginning reading to a high school student desiring private coaching in order to pass College Entrance Examinations. This range can be extended even further, so that pre-schoolers are sometimes tutored in perceptual training, language skill development, and in "readiness" programs, while at the other end of the spectrum, some college students require private tutoring to avoid failing a difficult course, say, statistics.

Reading clinics and Education clinics are additional avenues for tutoring, providing diagnosis and remediation, thereby supplementing, reinforcing, strengthening, and clarifying the child's classroom educational program. One important feature of these clinics is the interdisciplinary functioning: In addition to the teacher, the "team" often consists of a psychiatrist, psychologist, pediatrician, speech therapist, social worker, and sometimes an optometrist specializing in visual training. In thus dealing with the "whole child", the possibility of fragmentation, which might result from concentrating upon the child's performance deficits in isolation, is greatly diminished. These clinics are often located in the university, though private non-university affiliated ones also exist.

Services such as this (a private tutor or a clinic) should be regarded as supportive and should be welcomed by the child's school. Siegel (1969, 115) believes that:

> Teachers (and administrators) who are secure will not view the referral of a child for supportive services as an indictment against themselves for not doing their jobs adequately. This does happen at times, particularly, with regard to the services of private tutoring—"After all, if the school is doing its job, why should the child require additional teaching?" The secure teacher recognizes the fact that some children with learning blocks, perceptual disturbances, difficulty in abstract thinking, deficiencies in transference of learning and relatively meager incidental learning prowess can benefit from one-to-one instruction. The need of these children for additional specialized teaching is in no way a reflection upon the classroom teacher's capabilities.*

Even in the instances where children are enrolled in Special Education classes, tutoring should not, ipso facto, be ruled out for them. Often, despite the inherent individualization of a small special class, a given child may yet benefit from being tutored privately besides.

Recommending that the school administrator and teacher—of regular or special classes—not be defensive about suggesting outside tutoring for a given child is only one side of the coin. A great deal of care should be exercised to avoid prescribing outside tutoring indiscriminately. This could be a "cop-out", tending to relieve the school of its responsibility towards the educating of the child. The problem resulting from such a practice will be compounded in the case of poor families who would find it difficult to meet the cost of such tutoring.

One often hears the warning that private tutoring can undo a great deal of what the classroom teacher is trying to accomplish for the child. Experience has shown, however, that this fear is usually ungrounded, and that the extra instruction generally reinforces—rather than works at odds with—the child's classroom instruction. Obviously, the word "look" is the same whether the child learns it phonically or by the whole word approach! In retrospect, there are only a few instances wherein tutoring "differently" can confuse the child. Notable examples of these are: if the classroom teacher is teaching the child to write using two lines and the tutor uses one; if the classroom teacher is using manuscript writing while the tutor teaches cursive writing; if the classroom teacher teaches subtraction with exchange while the tutor still uses the old-fashioned method of "borrowing" from and "paying back" to the subtrahend. By and large, the number of possibilities for confusion is small, whereas the opportunity to corroborate is frequent. Moreover, a knowledgeable private tutor will ascertain from questioning the parent and child precisely what methods and materials are being employed in the child's daily classroom. This makes even more remote the possibility of the tutor "undoing" the classroom teacher's efforts; the private tutor should regard the information of what the child's daily classroom experiences are like as guidelines only, and use his own judgment as to when to repeat, reinforce, and explain the classroom instruction and when to begin independent remedial measures based upon the findings of his own educational diagnosis.

Besides the private tutor and the Education clinic, other examples of individual instruction outside of the classroom would include speech lessons, driving instruction, music or dance lessons, religious instruction (preparatory to Confirmation or Bar Mitzvah), etc. Many summer camps—for the handicapped as well as for the non-handicapped—provide individual instruction in the total camp program. There are some private schools which emphasize tutoring. The pupils are educated in small groups as well as in a one-to-one setting, and can either enroll in these schools full-time or attend them on a part-time basis.

Role of the Parent

The role of the parent in the tutoring of her own child is a controversial one. The argument is presented that parents are too emotionally involved with their child and, in the process of tutoring him, may do harm to his psyche. One study reporting on parental tutoring in childhood dyslexia (Worden and Snyder, 1969, 52) found that it produced ". . . anger, frustration, friction, negativism, loss of motivation and considerable family disorganization and conflict. . . ." Furthermore it was found to be completely unsuccessful in fostering any improvement in reading skills. To the problems found in this study could be added the possibility that parental tutoring can encourage sibling rivalry. Another point made by those opposed to parents tutoring their own children is that teaching of children should be left to the professionally trained teachers. Still another argument is that the child needs to spend his spare time in relaxation, recreation, and socialization rather than excessive studying.

The pendulum seems to be moving the other way in that a number of educators are now saying that parents have a stake in the education of their children and should often be encouraged to tutor them. The President's Committee on Mental Retardation

(1969) made specific recommendations to that effect. One participant (20) explained "the schools cannot do the job alone; the parents cannot do the job alone; we must work together." Another (20) said:

> Parental involvement in the educational process is minimal whether we refer to regular education or special education. This wasted natural resource is of even greater importance when we consider the disadvantaged child or the child who functions at a sub-normal level.

A third voiced his opinion, urging:

> Consider parents as partners in the educational process, *training them not only to work with the children, but also in many cases to master the task themselves.* [emphasis added] Involve them in planning, implementation, and evaluation of local education, and provide them with materials that help in educating their children.

Project Upswing, federally funded and launched in five separate school systems (Philadelphia, New Orleans, Los Angeles, St. Louis and Denver) has as its purpose "to demonstrate whether specially trained volunteers can effectively improve the learning performance of otherwise normal children when corrective service is available on a one-to-one basis after teacher referral and professional diagnosis." Phase V of this project is entitled "Parental Participation—Ongoing." In this phase, "parents will be encouraged to participate in the program to increase their skills in effectively providing reinforcement of school learning" (Journal of Learning Disabilities, 1970, 480-481).

What are some possible advantages of parental tutoring? One, of course, is the continuity and reinforcement of the child's classroom education. (It should be noted that a parent will be able to tutor a child far more frequently than will a private tutor since fees and travel time are eliminated.) Another advantage is that the parent, while tutoring, is in a key position to observe the child closely. In so doing, she may help in identifying a particular health or emotional problem, which might otherwise have gone unnoticed for some time, and can seek the proper assistance. Finally, the fact that this individual who cares enough to give her time and energy, fully and solely to the child, happens to be his mother, can be most reassuring to him, and can play a vital role in strengthening parent-child relationships.

How does one reconcile these two opposing views? It is very likely that the truth does not lie at either end of this debate, but falls at some point between the extremes. In other words, there are undoubtedly parents who can and should tutor their children whereas others should be advised against so doing. The latter, however, may reflect a temporary state rather than an irrevocable one. Siegel (1969, 125) explains:

> This is not to say that all parents are equipped to work with their children. Some, being too emotionally involved, become nervous, tense and hostile when supervising and correcting their child; the child, in turn, becomes more anxious and fearful. Through counseling, such parents can gain insight into their own feelings and learn to accept their child's limitations. The skillful teacher may be able to select a minimum of responsibility for these parents—responsibilities that are sufficient to make them feel positively involved with their children, yet are neutral, nominal, and psychologically safe. Many parents, however, are well-adjusted, able and willing to work with their child. The classroom teacher should utilize these parents' cooperation, energies, and attitudes.

The parent who is still not equipped to tutor his own child may very well encourage a different person (the other parent, a relative, friend, sibling, older child) to provide tutoring when it is necessary.

Another plan is to "exchange" children so that parents who are good tutors—but ironically not good tutors for their own children—can teach each others' children.

Now the notion of a parent teaching her child is not nearly so far-fetched as it might seem. If a mother reads a story or recites a nursery rhyme to her child, isn't this teaching? Which mother has not motivated her child in memorization and communication by reciting a line, omitting the last word? (Incidentally, this educational technique, which parents do instinctively, is quite sound pedagogically.) Don't parents usually praise their children's efforts in such activities as talking and walking? This, too, is a necessary component of good teaching. Even coaching such basic self-care skills as eating, dressing, and toileting are essentially educational.

In addition to these examples, many parents involve themselves in their child's education by supervising his homework, preparing him for his spelling test, listening to him read, or even trying to explain the "new math" to him.

Flowers (1969) believes that parents of children with learning disabilities can—and should—teach their children, but that being a "homework helper" is only one way (possibly the least important) of instructing; instead, the various activities in the daily routine of both parent and child can be utilized educationally. These activities are replete with opportunity for developing sensory and cognitive skills, spatial orientation and motor coordination. For instance, encourage the child to identify various tastes and smells while blindfolded. Let him cut a sandwich diagonally to make two triangles. Ask him to pair the socks after the laundry is done, thus building color concepts. Develop his motor coordination by letting him sweep the floor, dust the table and help put groceries away. Promote listening skills by letting the child attempt to identify various sounds such as running water, sizzling bacon, a bell, etc. Make a simple "map" of the neighborhood after going for a brief walk with the child. Teach him to follow oral instructions, beginning with single commands—e.g., "Please bring me a handkerchief"—and proceeding to tasks involving two or three commands. Teach him to match objects by color, shape, function, etc. and to categorize—e.g., "Name five vegetables," "Tell me all the musical instruments you know," etc. These everyday experiences promote training in sensation, conceptualization and coordination functionally, hence the child finds them meaningful and pleasurable.

Modern school administrators themselves (in contrast to administrators of several decades ago), seem to be aware of an emerging parents' role—a role which involves active participation and cooperation in the joint enterprise of educating children. Don't school principals establish lecture series and workshops in which curriculum specialists can explain innovations in methodology, materials, and syllabus to the parent?

The question of whether parents, in general, *should* teach their children is, in essence, a pointless query. The fact is that many parents *do*. One purpose of this book is to give all persons who teach one child at a time—and this includes parents—some means of becoming more effective in their teaching role.

Implications of One-to-One Instruction for the Disadvantaged

Tutoring programs are flourishing—and largely as a result of a responsive society's attempts to meet the needs of the disadvantaged. It is often pointed out that the major contributory sources of the plight of this group (as opposed to the underlying factors of historical injustices and the resultant psycholgoical "hurt") are inferior housing, poor job opportunity (especially the difficulty involved in "cracking" some unions) and educational experiences insufficiently relevant to them. Of the three, more progress by far has been forged in education because it is the one which is tax supported, hence the most vulnerable to criticism and the most receptive to change. In fact, it is probably safe to say that, in most instances, any current gaps between what the disadvantaged need from public education and what they get is far more a function of lack of definitive answers and funds than of racism-spawned disinterest. This statement is certainly more true of the institution of public education than of the fields of housing and the labor market. At any rate, programs such as Higher Horizons, More Effective Schools, Headstart, educational parks, increased day care centers, and bussing to achieve integration are attempts to bridge this gap. High on this list is the creation of various tutoring programs.

Characteristics. Why this preponderance of tutoring programs—as distinct from other possible alternatives—for the disadvantaged? Is the one-to-one setting uniquely suitable to meet their needs? Perhaps the answers can be found by reviewing the characteristics of this population.

Among the characteristics of the disadvantaged mentioned by Riessman (1962) are:

1. They develop a slow, "mulling over," cognitive style which can—but should not—be mistaken for stupidity (63-66).

2. They lean towards physical, concrete, "motoric" style of learning, rather than to abstractions and verbalisms, often doing better on the performance portion of intelligence tests than on the verbal sections (66-67).

3. They are externally oriented. In general, they are not introspected or introverted and are concerned much more with externals rather than with the "self"; consequently, they are more prone to view external forces as the cause of their problems instead of being given to self-blame or self-criticism (70).

4. They show an inability to listen to large amounts of adult verbalisms, being much more accustomed to responding verbally to their siblings—and hence to their classmates (84).

Black (1966, 46-47) enumerates some language characteristics of the disadvantaged: In general, they use a relatively small number of words compared with the amount of words they actually understand; the pre-schoolers do not know all the words used by the non-disadvantaged but conversely they know many other words from their own environment; they often do not know the names of objects and are particularly unaware that the same objects frequently have several possible names. (This is a direct result of their economically deprived milieu characterized by a relative paucity of objects.) Among the kindergarten classes, the disadvantaged children use a smaller number of words and with less variety than do the non-disadvantaged; they use less mature (e.g., compound, complex) sentence structure than do their more privileged counterpart; they learn less from listening than do others.

Black (1966, 47-48) believes that there is a learning pattern typical of disadvantaged children. They frequently learn inductively more easily than by deductive means (probably because economic injustices and/or outright discrimination lead them towards a basic distrust of their own judgment, and instead, fosters reliance upon an authority figure such as the classroom teacher). They are generally not given to the utilization of externals such as lectures or family discussions in "insight building" and have not had the normal amount of experience dealing with symbols (for example, the almost universal experience of children creating imaginary playmates is often discouraged by the disadvantaged child's parents). They do not usually value long-term goals, but instead want to make immediate and concrete use of what has just been learned. They are often distractible, finding it particularly difficult to "tune in" to the teacher's verbal communication for any prolonged periods of time.

Factors directly related to classroom behavior, according to Black (1966, 49) include: lack of familiarity with the "ground rules" for experiencing success in school, general lack of motivation to read, poor reaction to—and performance in—timed test situations, and a general non-awareness that adults, particularly teachers, serve in a "resource" role (i.e., one can ask questions and receive answers from them).

In addition to these characteristics, there may often be other problems which can be directly attributable to a low socio-economic environment. It is well-known that such factors as malnutrition, inadequate medical facilities, and poor obstetrics (conditions all too common in ghetto areas) can result in a high incidence of birth injuries. Many authors (Fite and Schwartz, n.d., Kappelman et al., 1969; Grotberg, 1970) believe that brain-injury and resultant learning disorders—perceptual impairment, hyperactivity, etc.—are more prevalent in poverty areas than elsewhere. Then, too, an impoverished environment is often accompanied by inadequate perceptual stimulation (Marans and Lourie, 1967, 27) leading, at times, to a poorly integrated nervous system, poor self-awareness, and possible withdrawal. In fact, Hallahan (1970) has pointed out that some of the minimal brain-injured traits—distractibility, hyperactivity and impulsivity—are found in many disadvantaged children as well.

There are numerous possible causes for the disproportionately large number of learning disorders among the disadvantaged (Kappelman et al., 1969). Among those mentioned are perceptual dysfunction, mental retardation, "pseudo retardation" (reflecting the relatively low verbal/high performance style of the culturally deprived), and emotional and educational immaturity.

Why tutoring helps. There are many merits which tutoring holds for the disadvantaged. Any handicapping conditions arising from the preceding characteristics (a slow, "mulling over" cognitive style; an inability to tolerate large doses of adult verbalism; a basic distrust of their own judgment and giving undue deference to authority figures; a motoric style of response in lieu of a leaning towards abstractions and language, etc.) generally require many of the therapeutic elements (listed on page 12) found primarily in the one-to-one teaching setting. For instance, the curriculum is "tailor-made"; the teacher can observe the child more closely and "know" him more fully; greater flexibility is possible; distractibility can be reduced; tutoring can be therapeutic and ego-building; in many instances, the teacher can see the child in his milieu, and work closely with the parent, etc. The structure recommended for hyperactive and perceptually impaired children, and also for the disadvantaged, can be applied more easily to a tutoring session than to a classroom. Similarly, learning disorders require individual remediation, and emotional problems are often lessened by a teacher's psychological support. Both amelioratives are easier to provide when teaching the child individually.

This is not to say that all disadvantaged children need tutoring. Even among those requiring this educational setting, tutoring in the majority of the cases is recommended to augment—and not take the place of—the regular classroom experience. Finally, this one-to-one instruction is not deemed to be necessary for the disadvantaged indefinitely. Instead it is viewed as an ego-building force and as compensatory education. Once the child "catches up," he no longer needs the extra help.

Various tutoring programs in different parts of the country report significant gains to the disadvantaged, both as tutor and tutee:

Where high school students of one color tutor students of another color, better race relations are established; in addition, such a program can serve to involve the high school pupil directly in community activity (New York Times, February 4, 1970, 23). In a Headstart Follow Through Program at the University of Florida, it was demonstrated that parents, when given professional guidance in engaging in readiness educational activities with their pre-school child, gained in feelings of competence and self-worth (New York Times, February 3, 1970, 46).

Among the aims of New York City's Homework Helper Program (a program involving 1,500 tutors composed of tenth, eleventh, and twelfth grade local high school students, as well as some from local colleges, and 4,500 tutees composed of fourth, fifth, and sixth graders functioning below grade level) were: to encourage high school students (by means of the economic assistance of a tutor's salary) to remain in school, to give the tutors the opportunity to experience success, and to provide career guidance experiences for them. The tutees profited from the program by receiving aid in basic skill improvement, help in developing effective study habits, and encouragement to complete their homework. They benefited because of the emotional and psychological support from their tutors. It was pointed out that "pupils relate naturally to their tutors because of their common interest and concern" (Barratta, 1969).

In a summer program in Timonium, a suburb of Baltimore, in which 220 institutionalized delinquent teenagers tutored public school children, ages six to thirteen, the following tutor gains were cited (Pfeil, 1969): developments of insights into themselves, probably to a higher degree than professional guidance counseling could have provided; growth in self-discipline such as punctuality and refraining from smoking in their charge's presence; desire to maintain appropriate class conduct when their own institution's school reopened; more favorable self-esteem since they felt needed by both the faculty and the children; improvement in their own reading ability; decision to pursue teaching as a career. The tutees benefited greatly from the extra attention and affection as well as from the lessons. It was further found that many of the children chose tutors of another race.

Student nurses from disadvantaged areas attending a community college were tutored in the biological sciences by proficient college students (Glanzrock, 1969). The individual instruction effected gains in academic achievement and the impact was greater as the extent and/or duration of tutoring increased.

The major benefits tutoring holds for the disadvantaged can be summarized:

1. Tutoring is compensatory (providing the something "extra"—that is, remediation—to counterbalance some of the social, economic, and experiential deprivation.)

2. It is flexible. For example, the teacher can adapt to the language and listening style of the child while gradually—and *gently*—guiding him towards more verbal and abstract cognitive modes.

3. It is supportive. The teacher's undivided efforts and attention coupled with the child's newly acquired scholastic achievement can be ego-building.

4. It is relevant. The teacher is better able to become acquainted with the one child alone than he would be were he teaching a group of children—thus learning the child's values, likes, dislikes, interests, aspirations, idiosyncratic language, etc., and glimpsing his milieu. In this way, the teacher is enabled to adapt, modify, and personalize the curriculum in such a way that it is rendered meaningful to the child, effecting, in turn, a more positive and intrinsic motivation.

Of course, all of these projected benefits of tutoring are only potential; they are theoretically possible, but simply setting up a one-to-one teaching environment in no way guarantees that these favorable results do indeed occur. There are many forces impinging upon this teaching-learning experience, some vectors militating against, and others mitigating in favor of optimal benefits. One of the most important prerequisites of the tutoring program—one which can help to make "what's supposed to happen" during tutoring actually happen—is that the teacher receive systematic, professional, effective guidance. There must be pre-service training and orientation. There must be ongoing observations, consultations and conferences between teachers and teacher trainers, and in-service training (including demonstrations, intervisitations, etc.). There must be evaluations—again, ongoing (initial, medial, and final)—so that maximum feedback and the subsequent refinement of teaching skills and teacher attitudinal changes occur.

There is an added factor in logistics which often enables the disadvantaged to derive maximum "mileage" from tutoring programs: Mothers of disadvantaged pre-schoolers were pre-service trained in a neighborhood elementary school specifically in procedures designed to increase the child's language abilities. This "home intervention" program not only helped the pupil being tutored but, owing to the crowded conditions of the urban community, was able to spread its effect through "Horizontal Diffusion" (a family close to the experimental one often began to copy the program), as well as "Vertical Diffusion" (a mother trained to teach one particular child in her family frequently taught a sibling as well) (Spicker, 1971, 635-637).

The paraprofessional. The concept of the paraprofessional has catapulted upon the current educational scene. What was once an innovation is now becoming a fixed part of the Table of Organization of many school systems. It is no coincidence that the concentrated use of paraprofessionals is to be found in special education classes and in depressed areas—after all, the pupil population in both cases needs something "extra." Federal funds have lent impetus to educational programs employing paraprofessionals.

The rationale for the use of these assistants is that it renders education more individualized: the adult-child ratio is cut; the teacher is freed to give more instructional time to children since the aide often takes over some of the non-teaching duties; in some cases the assistant works with small groups of children while the teacher instructs the remainder of the class.

Tutoring enters the picture here in that: (1) the presence of the paraprofessional in a relief nature, often makes it possible for the teacher to offer *individual* instruction to a given child, and (2) in some instances, the paraprofessionals, themselves, act as tutors.

The child benefits from the paraprofessional's tutoring in many ways:

1. He receives extra instruction and attention.
2. He is likely to "relate" to the paraprofessional, since both frequently come from the same socio-economic environment (this relationship can foster increased self-esteem and can stimulate motivation).
3. The paraprofessional can often help the teacher understand the child more fully, being able to fill in informational gaps regarding his background.

The paraprofessionals, themselves, benefit from teaching one child at a time:

1. Their self-confidence is heightened by any success achieved by "their charge." The feeling of being needed by the child strikes a vital psychological chord, and any signs of appreciation not only from the child but also from the teacher and the school administrator further enhance their self-worth.
2. They are usually a member of the team, working side-by-side with the teacher, attending case conferences, etc. This mingling and working cooperatively with professionals, coupled with the in-service training usually included in

these programs, can create within the paraprofessional an image (and a valid one) of professional or at least semi-professional status. This is particularly important in the case of paraprofessionals who themselves are products of impoverished environments and whose self-esteem may very well need this bolstering.

3. They are encouraged, in many instances, to undergo further training enabling them to become licensed teachers. The experience of working with one child at a time enables them to get first-hand, in-depth, clinical knowledge of children and provides them with invaluable data regarding their own teaching techniques. Should they, then, decide to pursue teaching as a career, their tutoring role as a paraprofessional will have provided a most useful training.

Diversification among the disadvantaged population. The foregoing characteristics and needs of the disadvantaged population apply in a general sense only. There are many variations, as evidenced by the diverse opinions of authorities in the field, the intra-group variability (i.e., the range of differences between any two persons within a specific segment of the disadvantaged population, reflecting the complexity and uniqueness of any individual), and inter-group differences (differences between the various groups of disadvantaged).

For example, a structured educational environment is frequently recommended for the disadvantaged, yet at least one author (Gordon, 1968, 71) warns that by structuring their classroom environment, ". . . we strangle the feeling of involvement that comes with creative 'experience' . . ." Riessman (1962, 72) however, believes that the model teacher of disadvantaged children will blend the traditional educational philosophy which emphasizes structure with the progressive approach of "learning by doing." He explains that the progressive system, by itself, stresses many of the tenets usually prescribed for the disadvantaged (namely, the physical, "motoric" approach; concretization; experience-centered curriculum). But it also includes features which are alien to their background and hence incompatible with their learning style (the general permissiveness, the focusing on the "self," the stressing of creativity, the prominent role given to play, and the relatively little importance attached to discipline and authority).

Mackler and Giddings (1965) discerned that there are many errors and dangers deriving from making generalizations concerning the disadvantaged. They cite various studies to show that, contrary to popular opinion and findings in the literature, many parents of disadvantaged *are* interested in education and desirous of their child's attaining good education. The authors view the anti-intellectualism usually attributed to the disadvantaged as really reflective of the larger pervasive anti-intellectualism in the country today. "Why then," they ask, "should the disadvantaged group be singled out as a prime example of anti-intellectual propensities when the majority of us are anti-egghead?" They also question (1) whether sensory deprivation is always a concomitant of disadvantaged areas and (2) even given the factor of experiential and sensory deprivation, must the same negative results inevitably occur for all individuals concerned. The authors believe that social forces and individual motivation account for extreme variability between subjects, so that success in one case and failure in another often occur under identical conditions of deprivation. They report that by visiting disadvantaged areas, it was found that many of the homes were comparable, in numerous criteria, to those in privileged sections.

Riessman (1961, 51-57; 1962) was quick to point out that there exist many "overlooked positives" of disadvantaged groups (e.g., the ability to express anger, the freedom from competition-induced pressure, less sibling rivalry). Moreover, he says some of the traits that seem negative and unfortunate, may in reality be strengths. For example, slowness in performing intellectual tasks might very well reflect care, meticulosity, creativity, caution, and unwillingness to generalize superficially, etc.—all positives. In fact, it has been noted that the pattern of charatceristics of the disadvantaged seem to coincide, in many ways, to the style of the highly creative individual (Riessman, 1962, 73). Giddings (1966) believes that the disadvantaged may have a real affinity for the field of science owing largely to their respect for the physical sciences, their physical, non-symbolic style, their notion that science can enable one to fathom the complex world and to establish some degree of control over it, their viewing science as being more relevant to ordinary activities than are the other subject areas, and finally, their consideration of the career opportunities for them in science. It is not coincidental that our national interest in science, since the advent of Sputnik, has led to increased talent search from among the disadvantaged population.

If there are individual differences among members within a given segment of the disadvantaged population, there are obviously even more differences between one disadvantaged group and another. No monolithism exists here. The teacher who desires to be truly effective with disadvantaged classes must understand and take into account differences between Chicano-Americans, Indians, migrant workers, blacks, Puerto Ricans, recently arrived non-English-speaking foreigners, Orientals, the Appalachian-type populations, etc. A participant in the President's Committee on Mental Retardation (1970, 21) summed it up: "Although group efforts are invaluable, we should have our individual differences among groups . . . we should avoid giving the impression that we have many common problems. I think we have one big problem: Poverty."

So there it is! The diverse opinions of the professionals. Intragroup variability. And differences between groups of disadvantaged. How can a teacher ever learn to take into account all of these differences? Again, the one-to-one teaching setting looms to the forefront as the ideal initial teacher training arrangement. By instructing one child at a time, the teacher can more readily:

1. experiment with blending the traditional and progressive approaches

2. develop a "sense" of the individual, and by probing, prescribing, evaluating, and refining, devise instructional techniques which, while suited for the disadvantaged *generally,* nevertheless will reflect the *individual* disadvantaged child's needs

3. become familiar with the forces (both positive and negative ones) emanating from the child's environment

4. develop an inquiring mind regarding value judgments of a given trait (for example, consider the tendency of the disadvantaged child to avoid self-blame. Is this a fault or a virtue? And more important, how can the teacher use this trait in helping the child?)

The knowledge gained, the sensitivity developed, the insight derived, and the attitudes formed while teaching disadvantaged children—one at a time—can effect the emergence of a model teacher in a classroom for the disadvantaged.

References

Aranov, Bernard M., "Reactions of Child, Family and Teacher to Handicap in the Child," in Doreen Kronick (ed.), *Learning Disabilities: Its Implications to a Responsible Society,* Chicago: Developmental Learning Materials, 1970.

Barratta, Anthony N., *An Evaluation of the District Nine Homework Helper Program, Title I Project,* New York: Fordham University, School of Education, June 20, 1969.

Black, Millard H., "Characteristics of the Culturally Disadvantaged Child," in Joe L. Frost and Glenn R. Hawkes (eds.), *The Disadvantaged Child,* New York: Houghton Mifflin Co., 1966, pp. 45-50.

Connor, Frances P., *Education of Homebound or Hospitalized Children,* New York: Bureau of Publications, Teachers College, Columbia University, 1964.

Dawson, Martha E., "A New Look at an Old Idea—Non-graded Elementary School at Hampton Institute," in *Pioneer Ideas in Education,* Committee on Education and Labor, House of Representatives, 87th Congress, Second Session, Washington; U.S. Gov't Printing Office, 1962, pp. 21-28.

Donahue, George T. and Nichtern, Sol, *Teaching the Disturbed Child,* New York: The Free Press, 1965.

Fenichel, Carl, "MAMA or M.A.?, The Teacher-'Mom' Program Evaluated," *Journal of Special Education,* Vol. I, No. I, Fall, 1966, pp. 45-51.

Fite, June H., and Schwartz, Louise A., *"Screening Culturally Disadvantaged First Grade Children for Potential Reading Difficulties Due to Constitutional Factors—A Preliminary Report,"* Hunter College Educational Clinic, Hunter College of the City University of New York (n.d., n.p.).

Flowers, Ann M., *Helping the Child With a Learning Disability: Suggestions for Parents,* Danville, Illinois: The Interstate Printers and Publishers, Inc., 1969.

Giddings, Morsley G., "Science for the Disadvantaged," *Teachers College Record,* Vol. 67, No. 6, March. 1966, pp. 435-442.

Glanzrock, Naomi (Project Director), *Nurse Tutoring Study of the City University of New York: Interim Progress Report;* Grant # NPG-326-01, June 30, 1969.

Goldberg, Ilse, "Tutoring as a Method of Psychotherapy in Schizophrenic Children with Learning Disabilities," *Quarterly Journal of Child Behavior,* Vol. IV, 1952, pp. 273-280.

Gordon, Sol, "The Mythology of Disadvantage, *"Grade Teacher,"* December, 1968, pp. 70-75.

Grotberg, Edith H., "Neurological Aspects of Learning Disabilities: A Case for the Disadvantaged," *Journal of Learning Disabilities,* Vol. 3, No. 6, June, 1970, 321-327.

Hallahan, David P., "Cognitive Styles: Preschool Implications for the Disadvantaged," *Journal of Learning Disabilities,* Vol. 3, No. 1, January, 1970, pp. 4-9.

Hechinger, Fred M., "Open Schools: They Can Be a Bit Too 'Open' in *The New York Times,* Sept. 26, 1971, p. 11.

Journal of Learning Disabilities, Federal News, Vol. 3, No. 9, Sept., 1970 pp. 480-482.

Jones, Joyce, "Dyslexia: Identification and Remediation in a Public School Setting," *Journal of Learning Disabilities,* Vol. 2, No. 10, Oct. 1969, pp. 533-538.

Kappelman, Murray M., et al., "A Study of Learning Disorders Among Disadvantaged Children," *Journal of Learning Disabilities,* Vol. 2, No. 5, May, 1969, pp. 265-268.

Mackler, Bernard and Giddings, Morsley G., "Cultural Deprivation: A Study in Mythology," *Teachers College Record,* Vol. 66, No. 7, April, 1965, pp. 608-613.

Marans, Allen E., and Lourie, Reginald, "Hypothesis Regarding the Effects of Child-Rearing Patterns of the Disadvantaged Child," in Jerome Hellmuth (ed.), *Disadvantaged Child,* Vol. I, Seattle: Special Child Publications, 1967, pp. 17-41.

Morse, William C., "The Crisis Teacher," in Nicholas J. Long, William C. Morse and Ruth G. Newman (eds.), *Conflict in the Classroom,* Belmont, Calif.: Wadsworth. 1966, pp. 251-254.

New York Times, Feb. 3, 1970, p. 46.

New York Times, Feb. 4, 1970, p. 23.

Orlick, Gloria and Ruchlis, Hy, *Guidelines to Classroom Pairing Reading Tutorial Programs,* New York: Book-Lab, Inc. (n.d.).

Passow, A. Harry, "Are We Shortchanging the Gifted?" in Joseph

L. French (ed.), *Educating the Gifted,* New York: Holt, Rinehart, and Winston, 1960, pp. 27-34.

Pfeil, Mary Pat, "Everybody's Somebody," *American Education,* Vol. 5, No. 10, Dec., 1969, pp. 21-24.

President's Committee on Mental Retardation, *The Six-Hour Retarded Child,* A report on a conference on problems of education of children in the inner city, August 10-12, 1969, Office of Education, U.S. Dept. of Health, Education, and Welfare.

Riessman, Frank, *The Culturally Deprived Child,* New York: Harper & Row, 1962.

Riessman, Frank, "The Overlooked Positives of Disadvantaged Groups," in Joe L. Frost and Glenn R. Hawkes (eds.), *The Disadvantaged Child,* New York: Houghton Mifflin Co., 1966, pp. 51-57.

Siegel, Ernest *Special Education in the Regular Classroom,* New York: John Day, 1969.

Silberman, Charles E., *Crisis in the Classroom,* New York: Random House, 1970, pp. 213-235.

Spicker, Howard H., "Intellectual Development Through Early Childhood Education," *Exceptional Children,* Vol. 37, No. 9, May, 1971, pp. 629-640.

Worden, Don K., and Snyder, Russel D., "Parental Tutoring in Childhood Dyslexia," *Journal of Learning Disabilities:* Viewpoints, Vol. 2, Number 9, Sept., 1969 p. 482.

Chapter II

Teaching One Child-Why?

You're alone with one child

You're trying to teach him the multiplication facts of the 5 times table. He understands the concept of multiplication—i.e., multiplying is a short way of adding identical addends. When you ask him the product of 9X5, he can count silently and accurately: 5, 10, 15, . . . 45. However, he has been trying to learn—or rather, memorize—these facts for quite some time now, but still frequently misses the products of 6X5, 7X5, 8X5 and 9X5. You try to point out a number relationship—"if you know that 5 fives are 25, then 6 fives must be 30." He agrees, but you observe that although he understands your reasoning, he experiences difficulty in counting by 5's, unless he starts at the beginning—he can't "think": 25, 30, 35, etc. You notice that when he attempts to give the product to the difficult multiplication facts quickly, he is not far from the correct answer. In fact, he is usually either correct or he misses by 5 (e.g., 8X5 is given as either 40 or 45).

If there were only a way you could help him become more precise! But there is! You suddenly see it! You take out seven nickels and line them up so that pairing can occur.

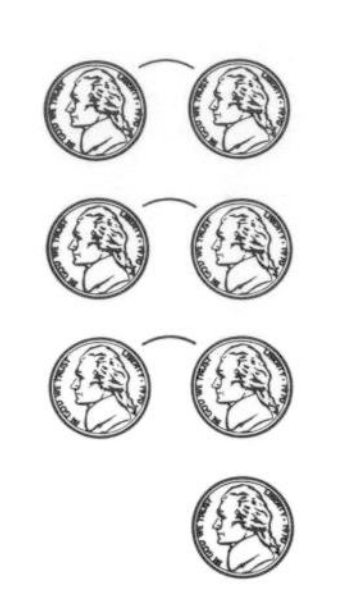

You point out to him that each pair is ten, but that the last row, having only the odd nickel, is five. The strategy now appears: If we are talking about an even amount of nickels, the product (since it is a series of tens) ends with a zero. If we have an odd amount of nickels, it ends with a five. From now on, when the child endeavors to determine the correct answer to, say, 6X5—and has it narrowed down to the possibilities, 30 or 35—the "6" being an even number and therefore requiring a zero at the end of the product, tells him to choose "30."

He "catches on" and seems more relaxed. In succession, you "test" him orally in those "5 times tables" facts which previously bothered him. He gives the correct responses much more quickly and self-confidently than before.

Because you worked with only one child, you were able to determine his level with a high degree of accuracy and to establish a definitive aim. (The specific aim, it turned out, was not to teach the "5 times table," but to teach him to select the correct answer from two choices: i.e., Is seven 5's thirty or thirty-five?) Moreover, you had the opportunity to devise, or at least select, an effective strategy since you were able—by doggedly keeping abreast of this one child's tactics and progress—to see clearly what he needed.

It is not unreasonable to concentrate on the pupil when evaluating the gains of various tutoring programs. After all, they were established because regular group instruction did not, either entirely or in part, prove effective for him. Teacher gains seem almost a by-product. However, it seems propitious to explore, and to explore in depth, the changes and outcomes (pedagogical as well as attitudinal) which the *teacher* experiences as a result of participating in one-to-one instruction. This is especially true if one desires to build a case for the mandated inclusion of some *individual* student teaching experiences in university teacher training sequences as well as in in-service training programs. (See Chapter IV).

There is a direction to this: the teacher will first hone, temper, and refine his teaching methods based on his intense experience with one child at a time. A master teacher, a clinician, may emerge, who can then translate his skills, insight, and expertise into classroom teaching. There is a paradox in teacher training curriculum. From the first day an Education undergraduate sets foot in his first Education course, we inundate him with the axiom, "Each child is an individual", while immediately proceeding to prepare him to observe, manage and teach *groups* of children. What happens all too often is that many teachers face the classroom seeing *one mass* of children instead of many individuals. To put it differently, if one seeks to understand children, he must first understand a child.

Note: It should be made abundantly clear that as each of these advantages is presented, a case is not being developed for all teachers to teach only individually; this would not be feasible, nor even desirable from any standpoint—financially, administratively, educationally. One group of teachers is not being pitted against another. What is being advocated is for *all* teachers to receive *some* one-to-one teaching experiences and that this will make them more proficient in the classroom. Certainly, one is not unaware of the invaluable experiences which classroom instruction offers the teacher: creating and utilizing classroom "climate"; developing group discipline; establishing and maintaining routines; utilizing "groupness" (e.g., competition as a motivational spur, sense of belonging, peer culture and values, socialization skills); attending to classroom administrative details (e.g., record keeping and reporting, selecting, ordering, maintaining and distributing teaching material); employing individualizing techniques (e.g., setting up two or three reading groups, unit method of instruction); supervising group health and safety; and planning for individual differences within the group. Above all, the sheer act of instructing numbers of children simultaneously is a most demanding feat, in many ways, more difficult than teaching one child.

Also, it would be untenable to hold that *all* experiences in teaching individually can be totally transferred to group instruction. From the standpoint of Gestalt psychology, which states that the whole is greater than the total of its parts, it follows that there is more to a group of children than the sheer summation of its individual members. In other words, there is a qualitative as well as a quantitative difference between one child and a group of children. What about classroom climate? Group dynamics? The need to "belong"? Peer judgment? Doesn't a child behave differently in a group than alone?

Finally one must not assume that all teachers will be able to make the transfer with ease. Often, teacher personality is a factor. It may very well be that a more introverted individual prefers teaching one child and could be ill at ease in the classroom, whereas the extrovert's preferred milieu might be a classroom of children. Moreover, the teacher being trained will very likely require some guidance and assistance from the practicum instructor (in pre-service training) or from the public school supervisor (in in-service training) in order to translate techniques and attitudes from an individual setting into classroom teaching.

Despite the absence of an across-the-board "transferability" from competency in teaching one child to teaching in a classroom, notwithstanding the variable of teacher personality, and even realizing that some pedagogical skills can best be mastered while teaching groups of children, it is nevertheless strongly advocated that the effectiveness of classroom teachers will be enhanced to a remarkable degree if their pre-service and/or in-service training includes the experience of teaching one child. Both settings—group teaching and individual instruction—combine to create pedagogical excellence; there is no substitute for experience in either.

Following are the advantages that redound to the benefit of the classroom instructor who, in the course of his teacher training, has been able to engage in some ongoing guided one-to-one teaching experiences:

1. Provides Maximum Feedback

In the process of teaching only one child, the teacher can "zero-in" on the most efficient and effective methods of instruction with much greater accuracy than is possible in group teaching. This is by far the foremost advantage that individual instruction offers the teacher. It is simply a case of necessity being the mother of invention! The teacher is able—indeed, is forced—to pursue the teaching of this single child tenaciously. In a classroom the teacher must often abandon the inattentive child, the poorly motivated child, the child who "doesn't get it," as he pursues group instruction.

Imagine a teacher with only one pupil: He explains something to the child; the child doesn't seem to understand. He says it again; the child still doesn't "catch on." He rephrases his explanation. In desperation, he whips out a crayon and an index card and literally "draws a picture" of it. He is forced to break the specific aim into its sequential components arranged in hierarchal order of complexity.

He sees immediately whether or not his approach is effective and is compelled to modify "on the spot." He learns—at times, with uncanny precision—how to regulate time dosages, employ tempo changes, utilize various sense modalities, when to choose failure-free or failure-prone activities, etc.

The key ingredient is feedback: How accurately is information about the learner transmitted to the teacher so that necessary corrections can be made? After all, that is the principle of servomechanisms. Input effects output. The ship (the teacher) is steering along a path (teaching a child). Is it the correct path (i.e., is he really teaching effectively?) Information about the course is fed back to its source. The ship either continues along the original path or else makes corrections based upon the feedback information. Let us compare a teacher of one child with a classroom teacher. Let us hypothesize that they are matched in their ability to "read" feedback and also in their willingness to change (i.e., neither of them is stubbornly defensive about his pre-conceived notions of what constitutes good teaching but is willing to consider different approaches provided that it can be demonstrated to him that changes are in order).

We have now arrived at the crucial question: *Which type of feedback is more valuable and reliable to the teacher, that information transmitted by the single pupil or that of the composite class?* Or, to ask a leading question, doesn't the teacher of one child learn more about the actual process of teaching (i.e., in the definitional sense of imparting knowledge and skills) than does the group instructor? In this author's opinion, there is no contest.

Imagine a teacher in front of a classroom: He explains something to the class. The feedback, for the most part seems positive. Let us say about 80% of the class demonstrates proficiency. He may not realize that the remainder does not understand. Some may be far too timid to ask questions, a few may be unmotivated, some may have learned to make eye contact with the teacher to "con" him into believing that they understand, etc. Besides, even if the teacher realizes that a few children missed the point, he may not have the time to help them. Finally, among those who seemed to learn the lesson may be many who *already* knew it. (In one-to-one teaching, the teacher can more easily differentiate between review work and new skills since it is possible to know the child more fully.) Thus, the classroom teacher is often fed back faulty information.

Similarly, the classroom teacher does not have the opportunity to perfect a particular sequential approach as readily as does the tutor. The classroom teacher presents step one; a segment of the class responds favorably. He presents step two; a segment of the class seems to grasp the point. And so forth for steps three and four. *But each segment may very likely have been composed of different pupils!* Hence the teacher is not faced with the necessity for refining and reorganizing his teaching steps.

The factor of success orientation is an important consideration in this discussion. Our culture, particularly, is an achievement motivated one. Quite apart from this culture-bred desire to achieve from an extrinsic (i.e., materialistic, prestige, social status, etc.) point of view, there is a deeper, intrinsically motivated need: stated simply, each one of us needs to feel success—as opposed to failure—in any of our serious undertakings. Certainly, our chosen vocation is a serious undertaking. Teachers, then, are motivated to be successful in teaching. Failure can be seen as an equilibrium upsetting force, the human organism striving to maintain equilibrium. So the teacher who fails at teaching, *and perceives this,* will make efforts (consciously as well as subconsciously) to improve his teaching abilities in order to finally achieve a more favorable self-concept (i.e., he will strive to see himself as a "winner" rather than a "loser"). Again, the teacher of one child can easily observe when he is not "getting across." He can then attempt to make the necessary corrections so that he can experience success. But the classroom teacher (as has been pointed out) is more likely to get *faulty* feedback of success, "perceiving" that he has taught well when, in reality, this may not have been so. His teaching methods may in actuality require considerable modification; however, since the data of failure are not fed back to him, his emotional homeostasis is not disturbed, equilibrium (or simply, peace of mind) prevails, and the needed growth in pedagogical savoir faire does not occur.

2. Develops Flexibility

Flexibilty, an important factor in individualization, can be more easily employed during one-to-one teaching than with groups. Flexibility includes the "tailor-made" curriculum (i.e., adapting educational plans to meet the unique needs of the one child) as well as the spontaneous exploitation of life situations when appropriate. Gallagher (1960, 49) feels that ". . . the individual tutoring environment in the present study [i.e., brain-injured mentally retarded in a residential setting] provided for the maximum flexibility in planning based on the specific needs of each child." He also points out that tutoring afforded the tutor maximum opportunity to deal with specific attention and motivational problems.

Flexibility implies that the teacher become proficient in observing the child, determining his overall as well as his momentary needs. If the teacher has planned a lesson or a course of action and the child is not "with it," the teacher, since he is there with only the one child, becomes skilled in modifying on the spot. For example, bring the day dreaming child back to reality, show learn to "hold everything" and cope with it in a specific way. For example, bring the day dreaming child back to reality, show interest in the creative child's ideas, clear the desk top of clutter, talk less. The teacher can best become skilled—and self-confident, too—in the ability to use a certain degree of flexibility while, initially, teaching one child.

Another aspect of flexibility is the readiness to try different approaches. If a teacher is considering the introduction of the I.T.A., programmed instruction, Cuisenaire rods, some aspect of the "new math," or is contemplating experimenting with behavior modification techniques, he will best become adept in launching innovations while teaching one child. Some reasons for this are the absence of distractions and discipline problems, the opportunity to observe, evaluate, and refine—i.e., the principle of "feedback"—and the chance to become skilled in organization.

3. Develops A Sense of Continuity

Many otherwise capable teachers do not do justice to their teaching performance—nor to their pupils' overall educational program—because of a lack of continuity in the total set of classroom lessons. It is easy to see why a structured environment—via continuity—can be more readily fostered in the education of children receiving one-to-one instruction than those taught in groups. If the child or his teacher is absent, the next lesson can nevertheless begin at the proper point. Pupil A in a classroom may suddenly become sidetracked by the noisiness of pupil B, fidgeting of pupil C, excitable mannerisms of pupil D, digressive offerings of pupil E, or the sheer proximity of pupils F, G, and H; when the break in continuity ensues, many children experience difficulty "getting back on the track." There are frequent interruptions in a classroom (collection of lunch money, loudspeaker announcements, visitors, etc.) which do not usually occur in one-to-one teaching. The varied needs, abilities and interests of the individual pupils in the classroom increase the difficulty of achieving continuity. The multi-faceted, prescribed syllabus seems more ominous when teaching a classroom of children and can very well serve as the rationale for the ineffective teacher to start and stop teaching particular subject areas at stipulated times, whether or not the lesson was grasped. In individual instruction, the parent can often be drawn in to insure continuity—not just in the lesson via homework—but in guiding the child into complementary life experiences, both formal and informal. Even if the classroom teacher attempts to make the daily lessons continuous experiences, since they are geared to the average child's abilities, it is likely that those children who have problems in learning will not profit from this continuity, having missed the original point.

Continuity can be subsumed under the general heading of "structure", and, as such, has its locus at the opposite end of the spectrum from flexibility. Although flexibility is an important aspect of a relevant educational program, it must be a flexibility which bends to meet the needs of the child, not merely a change in approach based on whim, poor planning, or administrative expedience. Indeed, if a choice must be made between flexibility and structure, authorities prefer the latter for children having difficulty in learning: structure can minimize perceptual distortions for the brain-injured, concretize the lessons for the mentally retarded, and set limits thereby enabling the emotionally disturbed ultimately to approach self-discipline. Hence a continuity of educational experiences is vital for the exceptional child; this in no way diminishes its value for "normal" children, who are equally entitled to meaningful, goal-directed educational experiences which are cohesive, rather than a disparate series of lessons and splinter skills.

The presence of factors militating against this in the classroom does not mean that the teacher will never be able to provide continuity of instruction there—it simply means that it is difficult to learn to do so. And one-to-one teaching experience is an excellent training ground!

4. Illuminates Pupil's Backround

In some one-to-one educational settings, it is possible for the teacher to work closely with the parents. Some examples of these are home instruction, individual instructional programs where the parent brings the child to and from the "class" (e.g., educational clinics, speech clinics, tutoring programs set up by parent groups), after school tutoring conducted in the child's home, etc. Teachers in classrooms often are at a disadvantage because they do not see the child in his home environment and because they may not have ready access to parents. In fact, critics of the public schools (whether from outside or within the school system itself) have pointed out that the average teacher's middle class background ill prepares him to understand, develop appreciation for, and teach effectively the disadvantaged child. Whether or not this criticism is completely valid, it is clear that a one-to-one teaching setting can, in effect, prove to be a teacher sensitivity-training program.

5. Provides In-Depth Experience With Exceptional Children

By virtue of the specific characteristics of the tutee population, the teacher of one child derives in-depth instructional experiences which are vital to his attaining the maximum level of teaching competency. This is true since the majority of children enrolling in individual instruction programs have significant learning or behavioral or educational problems. Many normal children learn a lot incidentally and tangentially; they learn considerably by themselves even with mediocre teaching, at times with no instruction! If a sequence is presented out of order, the child who is not educationally handicapped may yet be able to re-order it. If steps or experiences are omitted, he is often able to fill in the missing pieces—the so-called Gestalt principle of perceiving. Think back to your own childhood. Did a teacher have to explain to you the sound of the letter *t*? Did he have to help you remember the *S* sound by showing you that the *S* both looks and sounds like a snake? Did you require specific arithmetic instruction before you realized that if one is added to any positive number, the answer is the next number? Probably not. In fact, many children enter school in grade one or even Kindergarten already able to read and to understand simple arithmetical relationships. Of these children, there are of course those who reached that level because of over-zealous parents. But many did not need that push; they seemed to discover and learn by themselves. In fact, most children, should they encounter mediocre teaching, miraculously make the necessary educational adaptations so that they nevertheless, are able to learn (Kass, 1970). (Certainly, there are many variables which affect the likelihood of a given child's learning independently in a given situation. One important consideration is the inherent difficulty of a particular subject matter. A high school student studying a highly technical subject such as Music Counterpoint, Chemistry, or Statistics will probably not be able to grasp the subject by himself but needs a competent instructor.)

Now consider the population of children who are found in one-to-one teaching situations. There is usually a complaint factor which accounts for their presence in these programs. The educationally and socially disadvantaged, the learning disabled, the behaviorally impaired, the poorly motivated—all need *special* teaching attention and are not as capable of incidental learning as are the educationally *normal* children. In many situations, they will have to be taught specifically what most children learn incidentally. Even such cases as children in regular classes who enroll in after-school individual remedial programs or who need individual coaching to help them pass high school final examinations and college entrance tests may be viewed as having an educational disability (certainly minor and "localized" in nature); by extension, one might include gifted children who because of motivational problems are led to one-to-one instructional programs. In other words, the sheer presence of a child in a one-to-one teaching setting is often sufficient proof that he needs special help and is therefore a pupil who offers a significant challenge and a rewarding experience to the teacher.*

This view that experience in teaching the exceptional renders the classroom teacher more sensitive to the needs of and more proficient in teaching the normal child is receiving greater and greater recognition (National Society for the Study of Education, 1950, 5-6; Waleski, 1964, 13-14; Siegel, 1969, 143-146). The most illustrious example of this can be witnessed in the life and works of Maria Montessori, who began teaching mentally retarded children, then taught the normal, making lasting contributions in educational philosophy and methodology for *all* children. Current testimony to this belief is seen by the trend toward the inclusion of Special Education courses in regular teacher-training institutions. Similarly, there is at present an abundance of teaching materials, including complete instructional programs which were initially aimed at Special Education but rapidly found their way into the regular classroom. In fact, their brochures recommend them remedially (for the exceptional child) as well as developmentally (for the younger, normal child).

At this juncture, a key question emerges regarding the education of the normal child: Since he can learn incidentally, why should we seek to make him, also, the recipient of "good teaching"? Silberman finds Amcrican classrooms "grim, joyless places". This certainly would be so, for the learning disabled in the regular classroom frustrated by mediocre teaching. The point, however,

* There are, of course, exceptions to this generality. In some cultures, notably England, tutoring is more of an accustomed instructional mode for educationally normal, but economically privileged, children. The same applies to some American children of wealthy families or of traveling professionals (e.g., entertainers). Driving education, piano lessons, vocal coaching and other such special situations often entail (for optimal educational achievement) individual instruction, yet do not denote educational disability. Even here, there are many advantages which accrue to their teachers by virtue of teaching one individual at a time.

is that *unless teachers learn to teach more effectively, the classroom will be grim and joyless for the normal child as well.* We must not be content to exclaim: "Look how much and how well this child learned despite the fact that he was not instructed systematically." Instead, we should reason: "if he got this far by himself, imagine where and what he would be if he had received quality instruction." Interest, perhaps enthusiasm, enrichment (horizontally), acceleration (vertically), direction and a sense of accomplishment would replace the feeling of boredom, the status of non-productivity, and the attitude that "anything goes." Besides helping the normal pupil motivationally and psychologically, the master teacher helps him technically—from the sheer standpoint of subject matter—as well. The ability to learn independently in no way negates the value of professional instructional intervention. An individual may be capable of learning to swim or write or read by himself, but will undoubtedly be more proficient in these skills had he received expert instruction along the way.

6. Minimizes Discipline Problems

The teacher of one child is, to a large degree, freed of the discipline problems frequently encountered in the classroom. He can concern himself more with educational problems (e.g., How does this child learn? Am I reaching him? What modifications should I employ? Shall I work "around" his educational weakness or should I offer corrective drills?, etc.) since he is not concerned with group management and discipline. Often, the classroom teacher feels frustrated because so many of his efforts must be devoted to "controlling" the class. In fact, many beginning teachers resign or are dismissed due to their inability to exercise control of the class. These problems may range in severity from coping with the so-called "disruptive" child to merely effecting classroom management; regardless of severity, each situation must be dealt with. Long range philosophical goals notwithstanding, it is safe to say that the day-to-day disciplinary needs of the child in the classroom do not necessarily coincide with his instant educational needs and often work at cross purposes with them. In a sense, the classroom teacher can never afford the luxury of total observation of and involvement with an individual child since part of him must always be concerned with the other children and their management.

There are many facets to the question of discipline. The tutor is not completely free of this problem. In reality he is in an "all or nothing" situation. If the one child is motivated, conforms, has a positive attitude, and responds to the teacher, fine. However, if he is hostile, withdrawn, negative, if he balks, and balks completely, the tutor fails completely! He can not ignore this child and proceed to educating "the rest of the class".

Moreover the child who is a severe behavioral problem in the regular classroom is usually excluded and transferred to a special class; in extreme cases, he is placed in a one-to-one teaching situation (e.g., home-instruction, "teacher-mom" program, the crisis teacher). Hence, there is a likelihood that the tutor will encounter a fair percentage of behavioral problems among his tutee population.

Still another point is that groupness, instead of militating against, may at times actually promote appropriate conduct. It is conceivable that a child who responds negatively and inappropriately when alone with a teacher, might develop more positive behavior through socializing in a classroom—peer acceptance, "normal" points of reference, motivation through competition, increased sensory stimulation, are all key factors.

In general, however, teaching one child (although at times, one must learn to first deal with or teach "around" the handicap of negative attitudes and behavior) facilitates the emergence of the master teacher—one important reason for this being the absence of group discipline problems. Very often, the child who is a discipline problem in a group can be reasoned with individually. In fact, this knowledge is a well-known "trick of the trade" among teachers, recreation workers, and group leaders who work with adolescents. Also, successful experiences in dealing with a difficult child on a one-to-one basis can render the teacher self-confident in this area and provide him with techniques which may later foster competency in managing groups of children. Clearly, a single acting-out child is not as threatening to the teacher privately as he would be amongst a classroom of children. Besides, no "spill over" can occur.

7. Pinpoints Specific Deficits

In teaching (and observing) one child at a time rather than groups of children, it is easier to see not merely that the child fails, but *how* he fails. For example, a sample of penmanship does not in itself point out the source of the difficulty; watching the child *as he writes* can reveal faulty posture, incorrect pencil grasp, improper letter formation sequence, poor eye focus, fatiguability, etc. Similarly, observing a child working an arithmetic example, looking up a word in the dictionary, studying a spelling word, or using a ruler can indicate to the teacher the *source* of the child's difficulties. The teacher can then use this knowledge to devise relevant remedial techniques.

Individual styles can be studied and accommodated more easily in a one-to-one setting. For example, how should a teacher handle a period of silence following an oral question? Experience in individual instruction will show that the approach depends upon the child. A mildly cerebral palsied pupil may need a little extra time to enunciate his answers and it is a good idea to wait. Another child, however, may be so self-conscious and insecure emotionally that every second of silence is painfully embarrassing and points out to him that he is "stupid" for not knowing the answer. The teacher can help him by telling the answer quickly, avoiding questions with "high failure risk" for a while.

Children often develop strategies which virtually assure that they will not learn. Among those mentioned by Holt (1964) are:

1. "Reading" the teacher for unwritten clues signaling right answers (e.g., the teacher may speak more deliberately than usual immediately proceding the correct response choice.)

2. Not trying at all but waiting for the teacher's help. Holt (1964, 9) describes a child who wrote "mincopeat" for "microscope," and "tearerfit" for "tariff": "She closes her eyes and makes a dash for it, like someone running past a graveyard on a dark night. No looking back afterward, either." Another illustration (24-25) is the child who does not reply to the difficult questions, forcing the teacher to ask progressively easier ones; finally, the child knows the answer and states it. It is easy for the teacher to be fooled into believing that he is making the child think (after all, he is not telling her the answer). In actuality, the teacher has been "conned" since a close scrutiny showed that *the child did not mull over, become puzzled, nor even think about the difficult questions, but merely waited for the easy one.*

3. Mumbling an answer when one is not sure of it in the hope that the teacher will believe that the correct response was given; similarly, deliberately forming letters ambiguously (e.g., something between an "a" or an "o" when one is not sure which is correct).

4. Turning in written tests quickly, not because the work is correct and has been checked, but simply to end the

painful process of being tested. The child feels more threatened by the *prospect* of failure than with failure, itself.

5. Being preoccupied with producing answers rather than thinking critically and creatively.

Now, many of these strategies are subtle. They are probably subconscious. The psychodynamics of them are that they spare the child the emotionally painful experience of viewing himself as an outright failure: "If I did not really try, then I did not really fail." An individual instructional setting offers the teacher maximum opportunity to observe and recognize these strategies, and hopefully to cope with them in a manner which orients the child toward learning.

The tutor develops a sensitivity towards the tutee in two ways: he becomes skilled in following the child's train of thought and he is alert to the child's ego needs. Suppose in the course of a phonics lesson, the teacher says, "We have talked about the letter *'A'*. What is the next vowel on our list?" The child answers, *"B"*. The teacher has two choices. He can say "No, you're wrong," or he can say, "That's a good answer. I know why you said it. *'B'* does come after *'A'*. However, in today's lesson, we are talking about only the vowels. . . ." The second approach is the appropriate one. The teacher lets the child know that he "digs" him, and in so doing takes the sting out of a "wrong" answer. (This example was selected for illustrative purposes; it demonstrates rather clearly the advocated principle of identifying the thinking process which led the child to the incorrect answer and letting him know that his response is not devoid of merit. In this example, the reason the child answered *"B"* is rather obvious, and most classroom teachers would certainly surmise why he made the error. There are many instances, however, in which an incorrcet answer's etiology is not so obvious, but is locked-in to an individual's idiosyncratic experiences and interests, a particular thinking style such as a concrete language pattern or egocentricity, or the child's socio-economic milieu. In these cases, it is imperative that the teacher know the child as an individual.)

Often a teacher develops a preconceived idea that there is only one correct answer, the one he wants the child to say, and automatically—often, not too critically—rules out all others. Holt (1964, 16) cited an example of a child who made up the sentence, "I had a dream about the Trojan War", believing that the word "dream" can be a verb since it can illustrate action (the Trojan War does depict considerable action!) Without any explanation, the teacher told him he was wrong. She made three errors in this brief episode: she told the class that a verb *must* express action, she forgot that the word "dream" can be used as a verb, but her most serious error was in not grasping what the child was saying and thinking, thus leaving him baffled and frightened. The experience of teaching and observing one child at a time, particularly the opportunity to mull over a "wrong answer," may lead the teacher away from a rigid, dogmatic, "only-one-correct-answer" mental set and reciprocally towards really listening to the child.

There are many opportunities for this approach during one-to-one instruction since the teacher gets to know the child, is able to observe him closely, and has the time and flexibility to devote towards conveying to the child that he understands—and appreciates—him. There is a certain outlook, a knack, a philosophy, if you will, which the teacher must develop. Hopefully, the teacher comes to realize that what appears to be an error may actually reflect logic from the child's point of view and may very well stem from the teacher's ambiguous presentation. Moreover, even when the mistake is a genuine one, the creative teacher will still strive to identify the source of the problem (e.g., faulty prior learning; physical factors; elaborate strategies designed to avoid, but paradoxically causing, failure). This analytic style of critically evaluating an "apparent" display of failure to determine if it is indeed failure, of determining whether there may yet be some merit in an otherwise incorrect response and of seeking the *how* and *why,* not merely the *fact* of failure, can more readily be developed initially while teaching one child at a time and later transferred into classroom teaching.

8. Facilitates Observations

The tutor, rather than the classroom teacher, is in an optimal position for making observations which are total and ongoing. By watching one child, and one child only, the tutor has the opportunity to observe just how and when a child learns. One authority (Holt, 1967, VII) believes that when a child fails, he is using his mind badly whereas when he learns, he is using his mind well. In both cases, the teacher's educational philosophies and methodologies are created and refined on the basis of his knowledge, perception, and therefore *observations* of the child.

The teacher of one child is in a unique position to make pertinent and continuous observations. He can do so to a degree not found in any other educational setting, even the small special class. Holt (1964, 91-94) describes a lesson involving five or six mentally retarded teen agers, in which he was free to observe while Dr. C. Gattegno taught a demonstration lesson using Cuisenaire rods. The highlight of Holt's experience was in witnessing the precise moment that a particular pupil *saw:* "Something went 'click' inside his head, and for the first time, his hand visibly shaking with excitement, he reached without trial and error for the right rod. He could hardly stuff it into the empty space. It worked! . . . Many of us were moved to tears, by his excitement and joy, and by our realization of the great leap of the mind he had just taken" (93-94). The fact that it is possible to observe in depth only one child at a time is seen in this statement (92): "I don't know how the other children worked on the problem; I was watching the dark-haired boy." Or to put it differently, if Holt had allowed himself to become sidetracked in attending to some of the other children (although there were only four or five other pupils in the room and Holt was there as a pure observer, not as a teacher), his observations of this one child would have suffered.

The opportunity to observe one child and to record what has been witnessed can lead to skill in interpreting these observations. A notable example of this is Piaget who observed his own children, usually one at a time. His observations and interpretations have made distinct contributions in the field of educational psychology. His research and ideas, based upon the empirical evidence of watching one child at a time has helped professionals understand other children, individually as well as in groups.

The role of the teacher *as a clinician* is fostered by experiences in observing, recording, and interpreting the behavior of one child intensively rather than groups of children simultaneously. Later, this clinical approach and knowledge of child development derived at first from watching and working with children individually can enable the classroom teacher to understand children in groups and to teach them more effectively.

References

Gallagher, James J., *The Tutoring of Brain-Injured Mentally Retarded Children,* Springfield, Illinois: Charles C. Thomas, 1960.

Holt, John, *How Children Fail,* New York: Pitman Publishing, 1964.

Holt, John, *How Children Learn,* New York: Pitman Publishing, 1967.

Kass, Corinne, in an oral presentation, *Special Education Symposium "Prevention, Remediation, and Integration of Exceptional Children,"* EDPA Project, College of Education, University of Arizona, Tucson, March 7, 1970.

National Society for the Study of Education, *Forty-ninth Yearbook, Part II,* Chicago: University of Chicago Press, 1950.

Siegel, Ernest, *Special Education in the Regular Classroom,* New York: John Day, 1969.

Waleski, Dorothy, "The Physically Handicapped in the Classroom," *NEA Journal,* Vol. 53, No. 9, December, 1964, pp. 12-16.

Chapter III

Teaching One Child-How?

The principal thrust of this book is that experience in teaching one child at a time is the key to developing teaching proficiency. As important as this concept is, it behooves us to go further than simply describing the optimal teacher-training setting and extolling its virtues. After all, bringing a mediocre teacher to a one-to-one teaching setting merely insures a more intimate mediocrity! Therefore, it is imperative to consider the *how* of teaching.

It is no coincidence that the major portion of this chapter deals with sequencing, for this skill—the ability to select a suitable aim and to perform the subsequent task analysis—probably more than any other element or consideration, goes directly to the heart of effective teaching. (This viewpoint is recapitulated in the presentation of a model for developing teaching proficiency, chapter IV).

Obviously, all of the techniques and suggestions in this chapter are pertinent to teaching groups as well as individuals. However, *it is in the one-to-one setting that the teacher, initially, can best develop sensitivity to the needs of children and refine his methods accordingly.* In the interest of avoiding repetition, the reader should mentally apply this philosophy to all sections of this chapter.

SEQUENCING

RATIONALE FOR TASK ANALYSIS

Practitioners are beginning to demand from the educators a viable definition of "good teaching." All too often, in the past, research, professional publications, and college courses have left a void which became apparent when the classroom teacher tried to discover and utilize a "how to". There are several reasons for this:

A. The concept of the "whole child" can easily create an emphasis on diagnosis to the virtual exclusion of methodology. Meidinger (1970, 33) states that

1. college courses dealing with learning disabilities tend to minimize remediation while emphasizing diagnosis,

2. instructional technology should include ". . . the ability to set behavioral objectives, to do task analysis, to do educational programming, . . .", and

3. "this lack of instruction in educational programming skills is one of our most serious problems in the learning disabilities field."

B. An over-concern with the humanistic approach (psychological, social, and/or economic factors) often nudges out any real consideration for development of effective intructional techniques. Gordon (1969) explains:

"There are many good reasons for improving the living conditions of the disadvantaged; there is certainly no good excuse for an affluent society to fail to do so, but a concern on the part of the school for changing poor conditions of life should not substitute for a primary concern with the improvement of the teaching-learning process."

C. The frenzied pace with which one pursues innovations while automatically *and uncritically* ascribing the state of obsolescence to traditional alternatives can ironically lead away from the very answers being sought. (To appreciate fully the phenomenon of our present philosophical and psychological mood vis-à-vis the unparalleled accelerated rate of change, a mood characterized by a heightened awareness of the condition of *temporariness* in attitudes, values, relationships, roots, things, it is highly recommended that the reader refer to *FUTURE SHOCK*, by Alvin Toffler.) Rogers (1970, 48) asks, ". . . Is there a clear connection between innovation and academic achievement?" and warns of the danger in feverishly creating the new instead of "bolstering what is worthwhile in the old." Rawson (1971, 49) strongly advises us to avoid a ". . . smorgasbord of gimmicks, however novel and attractive . . . .", and instead, to approach teaching in a "structured, sequential, cumulative, thorough manner. . . ."

It should be pointed out that the above three points are not merely deterrents to effective instruction, but are *paradoxical* deterrents. After all, if one wishes to discuss "only" factors which militate against effective education, the list is well-known: lack of funds, overcrowded classrooms, bureaucracy, the "don't rock the boat" philosophy, lack of administrative support, disinterested legislators, "wrong" community pressures, some insensitive school administrators, some uncooperative parents, inflexible curricula, inadequate teacher training, etc. But who would ever suspect that the desire to seek diagnostic information about the child, the consideration of the child's socio-economic background, and a quest for new educational approaches, can also retard the emergence of effective instruction? It is because these deterrents are hidden, disguised, unsuspected, *paradoxical,* that they are being stressed here. Throughout this book, these and other paradoxical deterrents will be focused upon so that the teacher may learn to become more critical of philosophies, ingredients and approaches which, although proclaimed to be beneficial, may nevertheless militate against quality instruction if employed unvaryingly, unquestioned, totally, and unmodified.

Perhaps the best way to arrive at truly effective instruction is to avoid esoteric constructs and simply regard "teaching" definitionally, that is, in the limited and somewhat confined yet specific sense of imparting knowledge and skills. Blackman (1963, 382) feels that the profile of the child's strengths and weaknesses in learning and perception should be matched with the learning and perceptual requirements of the task. Another way of stating this is to say that a good teacher will:

1. select a relevant and appropriate task,
2. know—or create—a sequence based on the hierarchy of competencies needed to perform the task, and
3. make the necessary modifications based upon the individual child's profile of strengths and weaknesses (e.g., concretization, repetition, multisensory approaches, small doses, provision for physical movement, use of "success assured" activities).

Selection of the appropriate aim and making the necessary modifications are directly related to our knowledge of the *child.* The sequence design, however, is related to our knowledge of—and feeling for—*the task.* It may very well be that a good approach in making a task analysis is initially to *forget the child and concentrate on the task.* Now, this is not as heretic as it may seem at first glance. First of all, we can never really forget the child since we have had so many child-oriented experiences: courses in educational psychology, child development and methodology, the practicum course, actual teaching, etc. It is merely a question of emphasis. If we get hung up on the child, that is on the diagnostic phase of prescriptive teaching, we may never get around to a consideration of the task and its sequential components. But, conversely, if we design a valid sequence, and if we know the child, the modifications needed will frequently be apparent; in fact, at times, *for special as well as for general education, no modifications will be necessary!* It is as though the sequence itself offers the child the structure and support necessary for effective learning.

Examples of Task Analyses

The following five sequences are offered as examples of task analyses. It should be noted that the aims are definitive ones; furthermore all portions of the sequences are directly related to the aim, thus eliminating meaningless digressions and the possible instrusion of extraneous activities. Finally, it should be pointed out that generally each sequence is a program (i.e., a series of lessons), rather than a single lesson plan—the possible exception being the sequence dealing with the "more than" or "less than" signs (Sequence III).

SEQUENCE I: AUDITORY RECOGNITION OF THE TEN VOWEL SOUNDS (LONG AND SHORT)

Behavioral Objective: Upon hearing a word that has any vowel's long or short sound, the child will be able to identify the sound.

1. Teach the difference between vowels and consonants (especially that vowels are made in the throat and can be held a long time—this is important for steps 3-6).

Vowels	*Consonants*
a, e, i, o, u (Do not include *y* at this point.)	All the rest of the letters
Sound is made in the throat.	Sound is made with articulators (tongue, teeth, lips, etc.)
Demonstrate this to the child visually as well as tactually.	
Sound can be said loudly.	Sound cannot.
Demonstrate this to the child.	
Sound can be held a long time.	Sound cannot be held a long time (Exceptions: m, n, r, l, s, etc.)
**Demonstrate this to the child.*	
Frequently change their sound (e.g., *a*te, *a*re, *a*bout, *a*ll, c*a*re, *a*sk).	Generally sound the same.
Demonstrate this to the child.	

*a. Tell the child that he will soon be instructed to cover his ears (by inserting index fingers in them), to look away, and that you will say a word and hold it a long time; you will then touch his shoulder; he'll remove his fingers from his ears, (look at you, if he chooses), listen to what you are saying and tell you what he hears.

b. Test to see if child's ears are effectively covered. (Ask, "Do you hear me?")

c. Carry out step a). e.g., say, "pay"; child hears "ay". Explain to him that you really said, "pay", but that the *p* sound disappeared quickly while the *ay* sound "stayed in your throat." Sometimes, having the word written on a card (in advance) helps the child to visualize what happens. Moreover, it tends to "prove" to him that you really said, *"pay"* not just *"ay"*.

d. Reverse roles of step *c.* (i.e., let the child say a word, cover your hearing, tell the child what you hear when he touches your shoulder.)

e. Finally, guide the child into feeling your throat–and his–when words are spoken and held, demonstrating tactually that vowels are produced—*and held*–in the throat.

2. TEACH THE PURE VOWEL SOUND RECOGNITION

a. Make a chart using key words.

Long Vowels ("alphabet name")	*Short Vowels (other name)*
ape	apple
eat	egg
island (Note: do not introduce *ice* sound yet)	it
oak	ox
use (Note: do not introduce *rule* sound yet)	up

Note: In the beginning, use the designations in the parentheses rather than the traditional "long" and "short" terminology. After all, these latter terms do not offer cues, and may confuse the child since, in actuality, the short vowels can easily be held just as long as (or even longer than) the long vowels. Thtre is nothing inherently long or short about any of the ten vowel sounds. The term "alphabet" sound can remind the child that these five vowel sounds are identical with the alphabet names of the letters.

b. Let the child hear the teacher say the pure vowel sound; child matches it with the key word. (First, try only two sounds, then four, later increase to the point where the child can finally distinguish the one correct sound from the ten possibilities.)

c. Later, let the child try to say the pure sound upon command. E.g., "Say the 'alphabet sound' of the letter *o*." (Again, start with only two possibilities, later increase to four, finally to ten.)

3. USE THE VOWEL IN A WORD IN WHICH THE VOWEL IS THE FIRST LETTER (E.G., *A*ND, *A*CHE, *I*NDIAN). TEACHER SAYS THE WORD, CHILD IDENTIFIES THE SOUND. START FIRST WITH TWO, THEN FOUR, FINALLY WITH TEN CHOICES.

4. SAME AS STEP THREE, BUT USE VOWEL SOUND IN MEDIAL POSITION, THEN IN FINAL POSITION (E.G., T*A*BLE, PL*AY*).

5 and 6. Same as steps three and four, but this time, the *child* says the word. (The teacher shows him an object or points to a picture, thus designating the specific word the child must say.)

ENCOURAGE THE CHILD TO HOLD THE WORD A LONG TIME, LISTENING TO WHAT SOUND IS "STAYING IN HIS THROAT," AS HE TRIES TO IDENTIFY THE SOUND.

(A hearing tube—funnel connected to a piece of rubber tubing—may augment steps 3-6, especially 5 and 6. The child is often helped by hearing his own voice in this way. A tape recorder may also be used.)

Additional Sequential Components

A. At first (in steps 2-6) the sound is exaggerated and held a long time; later, it is said more quickly (i.e., the words are said naturally rather than "held").

B. At first, the child tries to identify the correct vowel sound as the *teacher* says the word (step 3 and 4), then as the *child* says the word (steps 5 and 6), and finally as the child *thinks* the word (the teacher points to an object, e.g., the table. Child *thinks,* but doesn't say, "table" as he tries to match the vowel in the word with the key vowel sound).

C. At first (in steps 2-6) the child matches the vowel sound of the word to the key word using the chart (2a) which is available; then, the child is encouraged to associate the sound from memory.

Subsequent Experiences

Later, to make sure the child can use his new phonic skills in Spelling and Reading:

A. Teach Spelling rules concerning (1) silent e at end of word (e.g., tap*e*, not*e*) and (2) two vowels meeting (e.g., r*ai*n, c*oa*t).

B. Give selective Spelling "tests" in which the child spells by phonics (in nonsense–syllables as well as words).

C. Finally, observe the child's reading ability in which he demonstrates that he can apply his prior phonic auditory training and Spelling rules.

SEQUENCE II: CASHIERING SKILLS

Behavioral Objective: When a purchase of any amount up to five dollars is made, the child will be able to give the correct change quickly and accurately without having to resort to written computation.

(Although there is a trend towards using registers which produce the correct change automatically, there are still many businesses—e.g., restaurants, small stores, etc.—whose registers require "old-fashioned" cashiering skills. Cashiers, especially in the apprentice stage begin with the purchase price and "count up" to the value of the bill handed them, thereby arriving at the correct change. As the cashiers advance in skill, they "count up" only to the nearest 5¢, and then with lightning speed, they produce the rest of the dollar's change since they have become totally proficient in matching the two complements of one dollar—e.g., 60¢—40¢; 15¢–85¢; 35¢—65¢. It is toward the mastery of this last skill that this sequence is designed).

1. Mastery of addition and subtraction facts (1-10), especially all combinations of number 10. Stress speed and accuracy.
   a) Visually: e.g., Show child three pennies. He must say "seven" *quickly*.
   b) Auditorially: Say "four." Child must say "six" quickly.

2. Skill in counting by tens meaningfully and quickly. Use dimes. Teach that ten dimes = one dollar.

3. Same as 1, but use dimes instead of pennies (i.e., show child six dimes; he must say "forty" quickly).
   Mastery of addition and subtraction facts 10-100 (by tens), especially all combinations of 100.

4. Lots of experience playing store ("cash register," money, articles for sale, price signs). Use only dimes and one dollar bill. Items must cost exactly 10¢ or multiples of ten.

5. Same as 4, but use quarters, half-dollars, nickels as well as dimes. Items for sale are still to be exactly 10¢ or multiples of 10¢.

6. Same as 3, but use nine dimes and two nickels. This time, however, use sums ending in *5* as well as in *0*.
   I.E., Teach that 65¢ requires 35¢ to make a dollar.
   Explanation to child: "It is just like the tens, but *'one less'* because:

   6 (5) (Teacher says)
   3 (5) (Child's answer)
   ↳ (This accounts for *one* dime; therefore, the number of dimes (6 and 3) must add up to 90¢, not $1.00. The cue however, is the verbalism "one less" or "nine, not ten.")

   Sequence:

A. Visual (and tactual)–concrete:	*Dimes* *Nickels*
B. Visual—abstract:	65 + □ = $1.00
C. Auditory: Teacher says, "sixty-five"; child must say "thirty-five".	

Branching: Those who can't master the twenty subtraction facts (5+□ = 100; 30+□ = 100; 75+□ = 100, etc.) should, *in the beginning*, be instructed in "counting up" to the original dollar, thereby *discovering* the correct change. Massive doses of this activity can often increase the memory, so that the child will finally be able to retrieve the answer quickly.

7. Same as 4 and 5, but items for sale are now 10¢ and 5¢ and their multiples.

8. Introduce purchases of 11¢, 27¢, etc. Teach child to "add *up*" to the nearest 5 (or 10). E.g., purchase is 34¢. Child thinks:

   34¢
   35¢ (takes one penny for change)
   65¢ (takes appropriate coins for remainder of the change).

   Augment coin manipulating experiences with purely auditory and visual exercises (visual exercises to include actual coins as well as flashcards.)
   Branching: Those children who can grasp the complements ending in zero (e.g., 20 + □ = 100), but not those ending in five (e.g., 45 + □ = 100), can be instructed to count up to the nearest ten instead of five (i.e., 34 + 6 + 60 instead of 34 + 1 + 65). Continued practice in this method may help them learn to deal with complements of five, since they must "go through" the fives to get to the tens.

NOTE:

1. Each of the eight points can (and should) be taught in different ways: tachistoscopic cards, a variety of work sheets, oral exercises, games, etc.

2. Manipulative experiences (the physical grouping of coins); "Gestalt" recognition of groups of coins (e.g., one dime and two nickels make 20¢) and tactual experiences (differentiation between coins via tactual exploration) should be stressed.

3. For older children, this can be part of pre-vocational training. Concomitant and subsequent skills are: wrapping coins, filling

out deposit slips, taking orders in a restaurant and totaling the bills, computing of sales tax, etc.

SEQUENCE III: USING AND UNDERSTANDING THE "MORE THAN" AND "LESS THAN" SIGNS:

Behavorial Objective: When presented with an arithmetical "sentence," using signs, $>$ or $<$, the child will be able to read the "sentence" correctly; if the signs have been omitted, the child will be able to insert them, pointed in the proper direction, so as to make the "sentence" correct.

1. Discuss "more than" and "less than" functionally (e.g., "Look at the books in the bookcase. Look at the books on the desk. Are there more books in the bookcase?"; people in a subway train, people in a taxi; seats in Yankee Stadium, seat in this classroom.)

2. Discuss "more than" or "less than" using materials (e.g., two groups of pennies, two groups of blocks, etc.)

   a) at first, make the difference large, e.g., 10-2; gradually, decrease the difference.

   b) sometimes, synonyms help develop the child's concepts: "big bunch," "the most," "whole lot," "biggest* pile," etc.

3. Child places a cardboard cut-out shaped like the sign $<$ between two groups of objects. (This eliminates any distractions and digressions which could be caused by visual-motor problems if the child were asked to write the sign.)

*The superlative, though incorrect grammatically, serves to dramatize the difference in size to the child.

Cue:

The "mouth of the puppy" goes toward the biggest group of cookies.

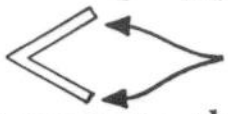

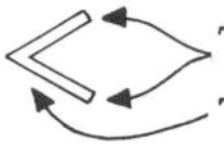

The big part goes to the big group.
The small part goes to the small group.

4. Try several pairs, placing the cut-out between the two groups of objects.
5. Write the sign (> or <) between two groups of objects which have been placed on paper. (If the child has difficulty writing the sign, he may use the cut-out's edge to help rule the lines; at any rate, success in steps 3 and 4 make it more likely that the child will write the sign correctly.)
6. Write the signs between two numbers. At first, the child works several sets under the teacher's supervision. Then he completes a worksheet independently:

Fill in the correct sign: < or >	
2 < 8	6 > 5
4 < 7	8 < 10
10 1	3 0

7. Practice reading the "sentence" from left to right (e.g., "two is less than eight." "Six is more than five.")

Optional activities:

a. Use the equal sign as a third possible choice.

b. Practice writing and reading the sign between algorisms as well as single numbers (e.g., $7+3 > 7+1$, $7+1 < 7+2$, $10+1 > 10$, $10 > 10-1$).

SEQUENCE IV: UNDERSTANDING PLACE VALUES (TWO-PLACES)

Behavioral Objectives: When shown a two-place number, the child will be able to identify the "tens" digit and the "ones" digit; the child will be able to perform a variety of activities (oral or written) demonstrating his understanding of place value (see step 10.)

1. Teacher sets up the number, using squared material, toothpicks and bundles of toothpicks, etc.

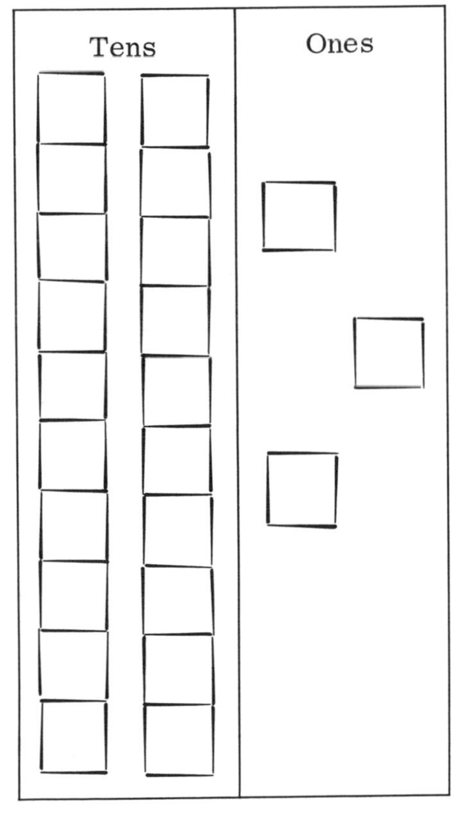

Teacher asks child how many squares there are. Child counts to determine answer. (Note: the child needs prior experience counting by tens as well as by ones.)

2. Elicit from the child and write down:

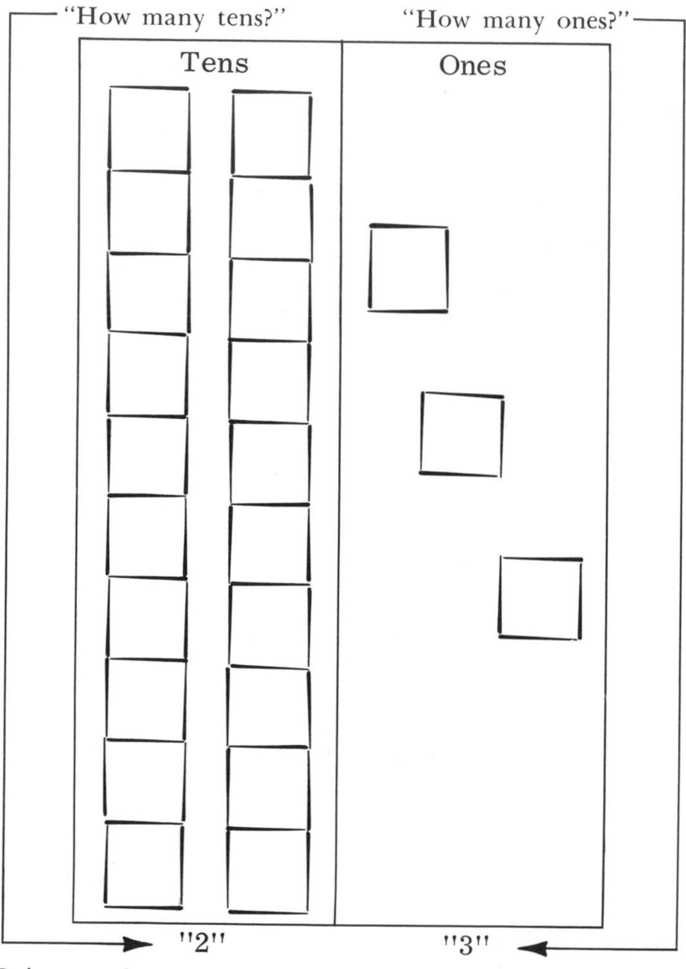

3. Point out that the answers to step 2 (i.e., *2 3*) look like 23!! (This is a very important step, since often, children recog-

nize—i.e., can read and write—two-place numbers before they are aware of place value. Recognizing the familiar is reinforcing and motivating.)

4. Do steps 1, 2, 3 with other numbers (see step 7).

5. Teacher sets up a two-place number. Child reads and writes the number. (Drill cards, pre-arranged with pastings of squared material help.)

6. Teacher reads a number to the child. Child sets it up. Teacher shows a written number to the child. Child sets it up.

7. Increase in complexity:

   a. other decades (no teens) e.g., 23, 31, 68.

   b. first decade numbers: e.g., 14, 11, 17.
   Surprisingly, although teens "come first" they are more difficult for the child to see vis-à-vis place value for two reasons: (1) the visual symbol *23* and the spoken *"twenty-three"* have the same left-right progression of tens and ones, whereas *16* and *six-teen* are reversed—it would be easier if the spoken word for the number "16" were "tendy-six" or simply "ten-six". (Some languages do not reverse all of the first decade numbers. For example, 17, 18, and 19 in French are, respectively, dix-sept, dix-huit, and dix-neuf—i.e., "ten-seven," "ten-eight," and "ten-nine") and (2) if shown a teen number set-up, e.g., one bundle of toothpicks and four single toothpicks depicting "14," and asked, "How many tens?" the child is apt to reply, "ten tens"—the concept of "one ten" being more difficult to grasp than "three tens" or "five tens."

   c. One-place numbers (e.g., 6, 8, 1); and multiples of ten (e.g., 20, 40, 50).

These kinds of numbers are usually easier for children to manipulate than are the other two-place numbers. However, because we have been emphasizing that each column will have a set—or a digit—in it, the child may have developed a frame of mind where he looks for a real number in each column. At this point, the experience of dealing with one-place numbers and multiples of ten focuses upon zero as a place holder.

8. Use other materials; e.g., bundles of tongue depressors, wooden rods. Dimes and pennies may require special instruction to show the concept that only one coin—a dime—can be worth ten pennies. (It is a good idea to begin by using stacks of ten pennies held together with Scotch tape; later, exchange one stack of pennies for a dime.)

9. Relate to sequence of numbers. Practice adding one more *one,* one more *ten,* two more *ones,* two more *tens,* etc.
   Note: Do not introduce concept of exchange—other than activity 8—during this period; no more than 9 ones or 9 tens should be used.

10. Use a variety of relevant worksheet activities. For example:

Write *Tens* or *Ones*

26	17	40
18	6	35
21	91	19

Put a ring around the biggest number in each row

6	16	61
30	8	19
41	42	43
36	9	10

Fill in the missing number

$36 + \square = 46$

$35 + \square = 37$

$26 + 20 = \square$

$6 + 23 = \square$

$\square + 12 = 17$

SEQUENCE V: DEVELOPING TOLERANCE FOR BODY CONTACT

Behavioral Objective: When touched by the teacher or another child (see step D), the child will not show any signs of aversion (e.g., cringing, frowning, crying, withdrawing, running away, nervousness, "tightening up," or verbal denunciation to being touched, etc.).

(If a child cannot tolerate contact between himself and another person, it marks him "deviate" to other children who do not have this difficulty. It often works at cross purposes to education since many activities—gym, shop, drama, arts and crafts, the "buddy" system of studying, etc.—entail some degree of body contact. It can even "turn the teacher off" since he may feel that the child is rejecting him. Most important, it signifies a basic unhappiness, lack of confidence, anxiety within the child which might disappear or at least diminish if his tolerance toward being touched by others increased. Or is the converse true? In any event, sequentialized experiences leading up to the ability to tolerate being touched, coupled with a positive mental hygiene attitude toward the child, seems warranted—an approach, incidentally, which has been used successfully with psychosomatic infants whose syndrome included this low threshold for body contact.) (Lourie, 1955)

A. Development of a state of readiness

1. *Have the child help you carry objects requiring two people.*
2. *Sitting at the table across from the child, use tabletop activities taking care to offer him aid only through a neutral object* (i.e., do not hand him a puzzle piece; instead, simply call his attention to it and push it within his reach). With a very shy or passive-aggressive child you may need to begin with parallel activities first, eventually getting him to aid you in your activity, before he can willingly accept

your offer of help on his activity. Be satisfied with the child's pushing or placing objects within your reach at this point.

3. *Play gross-motor games encouraging child to help set up equipment and allowing him great latitude in selecting games himself if he wishes.* (This is a good place to re-evaluate progress and gain clues from the child in estimating how much of the projected sequence will become necessary.)

4. *Sitting across from the child, encourage him to give and receive objects from your hands without having to first place them on the table.* Here, holding objects between thumb and forefinger is generally less threatening than holding them in the palm.

5. *Sit next to the child and repeat Step 4,* first regressing to Step 3 (pushing objects near child) if necessary for child's comfort.

6. *Sitting next to child doing tabletop activities, reach around and across and in front of him to pick objects that you need or that have fallen on the floor. Encourage him to do the same.*

7. *Have child work with objects you are holding in the palm of your hand,* (e.g., tracing rabbeted letters). *Reverse roles.*

B. Neutral body contact

1. *Have child take objects from palm of your hand.* These objects should be large enough at first so that he can get them without touching you. Gradually size should be reduced so that ultimately he must touch you in picking up objects, (e.g., small beads, buttons, etc.). *Have child let you reverse process,* taking objects from his hand.

2. *Using balance beam and climbers, ask child to hold your hand to help you balance while you walk and climb.* Exert only as much pressure on his supporting hand as you judge he can be comfortable with. Later increase difficulty of your tasks, so that you must rely more and more on the child's support to help you balance.

3. Concurrently with Step 2, *encourage the child to let you place your hand on top of his to guide it in a finger maze or in tracing letters while seated side by side at the table.*

4. When the child is entirely comfortable with Step 3, *blindfold yourself and have child help you in tracing activities. Reverse roles.*

5. *Have child lead you around the room blindfolded. Reverse roles.*

6. *Have child help you through an obstacle course blindfolded.* Set up course so child will be required to help you move both toward and away from the side from which he is guiding you, and so that he will also have to help you in climbing over, ducking under, etc. Have him hold your hand and "talk" you through. *Reverse roles.*

7. *Repeat Step 6, but directions should be given by touch,* (e.g., pressure on head to signal "Duck").

8. After you feel certain you have his confidence and trust in the above stages, *begin games that involve more movement along with minimal body contact* (e.g., Statues). Be sure to let him "do it to you" first so that he is clearly aware of how much movement and body contact is going to be involved when you "do it to him." *Take turns.*

9. *Introduce puppet play.* (This can be developed concurrently with Readiness and Neutral Body Contact Stages if

care is taken to progress from verbal, non-contact play to neutral contact play and to synchronize the stages with the preceding steps.)

a. *Begin by selecting a puppet for each of you.* Allow the child to choose his own and rely on his suggestions for choosing yours. Often your choice of a smaller child puppet is less threatening than choosing a mother or father figure; however, if there is a serious sibling rivalry problem, this is not the case.

b. *Engage in neutral conversations through the puppets.*

c. *Have puppets engage in activities where touching or holding is a natural outcome* (e.g., leading baby brother to the store, mother rocking baby).

C. Indirect contact, both positively and negatively valenced

1. *Develop the puppets' characters and relationships through conversations until affectionate and/or hostile-aggressive behaviors can be introduced in a situation reasonable for the puppets' characters.* Take care that emotionally loaded gestures are of short duration, of minimal intensity, and as nonthreatening as possible.

2. *Gradually build up the child's tolerance for interaction between the puppets until he can not only receive but express strong feelings through the puppets.*

D. Direct body contact

1. *Introduce hand-slapping games and arm wrestling going gently at first, and only gradually increasing your resistance and aggressiveness.* At the same time encourage gradual build-up of resistance and aggression on the child's part.

2. *Introduce leg-wrestling, elephant walking, wheel-barrow walking, etc.* Note that some activities now are competitive while others are cooperative.

3. *Introduce pillow fighting.* Be sure to agree on limits of space, time, and rules including a definite emergency stop signal. (Pillow fighting is technically indirect contact, but experience has shown that it makes an excellent and at times necessary bridge between hand-arm contact and full body contact.)

4. *If child is young enough or sufficiently regressed, this is a good time to encourage lap-sitting and cuddling.* This step is one that may need delaying until the child can be comfortable exchanging symbolically negative competitive communication, (e.g., play wrestling). Timing of this step must be left to the teacher's sensitive discretion and clinical judgment.

5. *Introduce "play-wrestling."* This must be structured at a time and in such a way that the child is secure in his conviction that the activity is "just for fun." Thus this stage should never be initiated on a day when the child is already upset and feeling hostile. Later, with proper structuring, he can be encouraged to work off debilitating hostility in this fashion.

6. Hand-holding while walking or sitting and putting your arm around the child's shoulders have been purposely omitted. These are highly personal contacts for many children, even more so than body contact games. Some children like these exchanges of friendship early; some never feel comfortable. This is another phase requiring the teacher's judgment.

Additional Sequential Components

A. Ideally, a teacher would incorporate the sequence into his general approach and attitude toward a given child. He would pick his spots during each session for casually augmenting whatever step the child was on at the time, so that a particular phase actually permeated the sessions on an attitudinal level. Certainly one would not expect to call the child's attention either by gesture or word that indicated, "O.K., Charlie, now it's Practice Touching Time." Flipping the switch on and off so abruptly would in all likelihood cause the child some very distorted perceptions and feelings, to say the least.

B. The teacher who needs more structure can set aside in his own mind (never overtly to the child) a short, but definite, period for introducing a new phase. Then he could spread out "practice" during the session whenever the situation permitted. A good time for a very angry, passive-aggressive child is at the beginning of a session. It often frees him to function better in the standard learning process. This is especially true of the effectiveness of the stages involving greater release of aggression.

C. Length of time spent should range from very short to longer and longer as the child evidences extension of tolerance. Time in minutes is not applicable here; the teacher must watch for cues from the child and operate on his "inner timetable." At major stage shifts (e.g., from neutral to indirect contact) the length of time spent may need to be reduced and gradually built up again. *Always the child is the barometer*—not how many days are left in the term or year!

D. Intensity and depth of behavior are controlled by the teacher's judgment of how much the child can tolerate at any one time. The teacher must be very careful to take his cues here from the child. Allowing him to "go too far" will only escalate the anxieties of an already anxious child.

E. Position of teacher in relation to the child ranges from distant to body contact. The teacher must himself be comfortable, casually working through various stages. Otherwise he may make the child feel he is creeping up on him.

F. Degree of support and reassurance ranges from total support at the beginning to very little or none at all at the end of the sequence. The degree depends on the needs of the child. A session should always conclude with a reinforcement of your supportive role. Recap any hostile behavior, getting the child to talk about how he felt then and now if possible. In other words, put the cork back in the bottle for him.

G. Regression to a need for greater support may occur as each new phase is introduced. Work on that particular step should continue until the child is entirely comfortable before proceeding to the following step. Unexpected regressions in degree of support needed should be carefully analyzed for clues that you are working on *your* timetable rather than *his.*

Criteria for Developing an Effective Task Analysis

When instructional sequences are needed, they are usually developed "on the spot." The teacher senses that a given educational aim is too broad to be presented in its entirety and so proceeds to break it down into its sequential components. He generally does this "by ear" without benefit of guidelines. It is possible, however, to draw upon samples of proven effective sequences in order to formulate criteria for the construction of other ones. The following considerations can prove helpful to teachers as they endeavor to devise as yet unwritten instructional sequences:

1. The aim of the sequence should be well-defined and somewhat limited rather than general. Aims such as understanding the grid system of a map, looking up a word in a dictionary, forming

the plural of nouns, using a scissor, telling time, etc. are manageable and not as unwieldy and unbounded as developing appreciation of literature, instilling an attitude of inquiry, learning to respect honest differences of opinion, or developing esthetic interests. It is not coincidental that Blackman (n.d.), in describing a typical day in the future when computers will be employed by the teacher in matching a task's requirements with the child's profile of learning strengths and weaknesses, chooses as an illustration of the task the very modest aim of learning to write the numeral "1"!

It is possible for some aims to be educationally oriented, whereas others will be psychologically based. Granted, the latter variety (e.g., increasing attention span; reducing disorganization; eliminating a nervous habit such as rocking; teaching a child to make eye contact when spoken to; etc.), possibly because they go directly to behavior and personality, may at first glance seem infinitely more significant than the educational aims (e.g., developing place value concept; grasping a strategy for auditory discrimination between long and short vowels; etc.). It is precisely because these "educational" aims *seem* so relatively unimportant that we tend to neglect them. Yet, aren't these aims the very mortar of the education edifice? Don't children still need to learn reading, writing and arithmetic? Shouldn't teachers be concerned with the most effective means of instructing children in these subjects?

The fact is that there is no sharp line of demarcation between educational and psychological objectives. If a child learns to read better, some of the consequences may be that he finds school more pleasurable, anxiety is reduced, frustration lessened and self-esteem heightened. Conversely, if the teacher could succeed (by some other means) in making him less tense and more self-confident, the child would probably perform—that is, *learn*—better. Certainly such "behavioral" items as increased attention and impulse control are totally relevant to the matter of mastering subject skills.

In short, a child must learn to learn, but he must also learn penmanship and spelling. It would be a shame if, in our zeal to achieve the former (possibly because of the scientific aura which we attach to psychological rather than to educational objectives), we overlook the latter.

2. The behavioral objective must be an observable one. (The term "behavioral objective" refers to either psychological or educational goals, the point being that *whatever* goals we are seeking for the child, there should be some clear way whereby he can demonstrate his newly acquired—that is, *learned*—prowess.) This concept of "observability" is by no means a picayune one. Granted, mental activity as such is not directly observable and hence not measurable; one must stipulate, therefore, an observable activity which *can stand for* those processes which, themselves, cannot be witnessed. (We cannot see electricity, but we can observe, measure, and control the *effects* of electricity.) For if a child does absolutely nothing observable following instruction, how can we be sure that he has learned? Thinking—and teaching—in terms of observable behavioral goals commit the teacher to a high level of precision, while providing the means for evaluation and the subsequent refinement of pedagogical techniques.

The instructional objective must not only be an observable one; it must be precisely stated or written. "To learn the alphabet" is not nearly so exact as "to recognize all of the capital printed letters and be able to read them; to be able to recite them in sequence beginning with any letter; to be able to respond correctly—orally or in writing—to 'What letter comes before (or after) any given letter.' " "To become familiar with the artistic style of Van Gogh" is neither an observable nor a precisely stated instructional objective. "When presented with a set of pictures, some of which are by Van Gogh, the student will be able to identify the works of Van Gogh" is much more exact. It tells what the pupil is expected to *do* following instruction.

The astute reader may at this point question the wisdom of reducing *all* educational goals to behaviors which involve performance. What about attitudes? Appreciations? Personality development? Creativity? And how about feelings? Indeed, there are other aspects to education than simply the "imparting of knowledge" theme. So it follows that there are other evaluative instruments in addition to the clearly observable "performable" objectives. Certainly, the teacher's "sensings" and instincts about the growth of the child, the parent's anecdotal reports of behavioral changes outside of school, gradual and therefore almost imperceptible changes in values and preferences, the child's subjective reports of his feelings, "body language" communications are all valid—though difficult to read—signs. In the long run, the impression that a child makes on the teacher and others is paramount. To put it differently, *how he seems* is possibly more important than *what he does*. Even here, however, there is a sequence: Before a child can truly develop appreciation of Mozart, (not a readily observed behavioral objective), he will learn to recognize Mozart's music and will be able to differentiate it from that of other composers (an observable behavior). The complete, effective teacher will become skilled in the sequencing of tasks and in the stipulation of observable behaviorable objectives *but will be able to view these in perspective* (See Chapter IV).

3. The number of steps must not be so large* as to overwhelm the teacher; yet the gaps must be sufficiently narrow to allow the

* The body contact tolerance sequence has many steps; however, the organization (the four major stages A, B, C and D, and the logical subdivisions) clarifies rather than overwhelms. It would have been possible to shorten this sequence, but because the aim is such an intriguing one and the subject matter is psychologically rather than educationally oriented (and therefore less familiar to the average classroom teacher), it was presented in this complete form.

I am indebted to Mrs. Betty Wallwork, Coordinator of Learning Disabilities Center in Los Alamos Public Schools, New Mexico who, while enrolled as a student in a special education seminar conducted by me at the University of New Mexico, Albuquerque, New Mexico (summer session, 1970) designed and wrote this sequence and granted permission for its publication.

teacher to gain a footing and to see how to proceed from step to step.

4. Generally, the increasing difficulty of each step should be visible and able to pass the test of face validity. The steps should be so arranged that when the student experiences difficulty at one level, practice at the level immediately preceding is often indicated. Some examples follow: *Sequence II, Step 3* — A child may very well be able to handle complements of $1.00 ending in zero only (since no exchanging is necessary), but not those which end in five (step 6). *Sequence III, Step 3* — Placing the sign is an easier dexterity task than (step 5) writing it; also, placing a sign between two groups of actual objects is an easier conceptual task than placing it between two written numbers (Step 4). *Sequence V* — The readiness steps in Section A are clearly less threatening to a child who cannot tolerate body contact than are those in Section B which, in turn, are less threatening than those in Sections C and D.

Although the sequential components are often arranged in the order of increasing complexity, there are exceptions in which an earlier step is more difficult for the pupil. Consider the task of fraction division, $\frac{A}{B} \div \frac{C}{D}$. Disregard conceptual considerations, such as the fact that multiplication—and not division—has the commutative property, and simply focus on the operational steps. Pupils are more apt to encounter difficulty in the first step—changing $\frac{A}{B} \div \frac{C}{D}$ to $\frac{A}{B} \times \frac{D}{C}$ — than in the second step of multiplying numerators and denominators, $\frac{AD}{BC}$. A *primary* requirement of a valid sequence, then, is that a *given step prepare the learner for the next step.*

5. Some instructions to the teacher are necessary, yet the specific methodology should not be spelled out. (The teacher should have

considerable latitude in selecting materials, methods, modalities, time dosages, length and types of drill, etc.) By getting to "know" the child, the teacher will be able to make appropriate modification wherever necessary.

Even learning theories can be accommodated while utilizing instructional sequences. Indeed, the whole field of behavior modification demands a knowledge of sequence. Operant conditioning, in shaping via approximation, requires that the learner have the task sequentialized for him. Contingency management, while seeming to stress the reward aspect of behavior modification, certainly involves, in addition, an aim selection and a step-by-step approach.

An amazing paradox emerges. Although courses in educational methodology should emphasize the sequentialized approach, sequencing, in itself, is not a method. Essentially, a task analysis creates a set of ordered sub-goals, *but any of the steps can be taught in a variety of ways.* The choice of method (including type and frequency of reward) is left open-ended, so that the teacher can exercise his own judgment.

6. General areas of difficulty should be anticipated and the suggested coping strategies incorporated into the sequence. Viz., the intentional omission at first of "y" as a vowel and initially avoiding the terminology "long" and "short" vowels (Sequence I); recognizing that the first decade numbers (e.g., 16, 12, 15), though having "only one ten", are nevertheless more difficult to understand in terms of place value than are the higher decade numbers, and therefore not beginning with them simply because "one ten" come before "two tens" or "three tens" (Sequence IV).

7. In attempting to design a sequence for a specific aim, the teacher must not feel that there is only one set of steps which will satisfy the requirements of the task. It is likely that ten educators,

each asked to design a single task analysis, will turn in ten different sets of sequential steps. We must think divergently rather than convergently. In other words, we are after an approach rather than the single correct "answer". For example, in Sequence V, we could quite validly have introduced such activities as applying a band-aid to the child, taking turns making slings and splints during a lesson in first aid, playing tag, applying makeup for a play, helping the child to swim or float, etc., in our effort to increase his threshold level for physical contact.

8. Great care should be taken with the layout itself, lest the reader find it overwhelming, similar to the imponderables found in the printed instructions in some of the commercial assembly kits. The points should be numbered rather than in essay form; explanations and examples can be helpful; additional sequential components and subsequent experiences (Sequences I and V), optional activities (Sequence III), or overall explanatory notes (Sequence II) should follow the steps rather than be included in them. Some times, it helps if the "heart" of the sequence is capitalized to differentiate it visually from the introductory and the remaining steps (see the Phonics sequence—steps 2, 3, and 4).

If each situation were unique, each teacher would have to create a new sequence for each child and for every occasion. Fortunately, one does profit from experience. A sequence employed successfully with one child may very well be entirely valid for another. A task analysis developed by one teacher may often be used advantageously by other teachers as well. Hopefully, sequences will be designed, written, used, stored, retrieved, and used again—processes involving teachers, supervisors, principals, consultants, itinerant and resource room teachers, educators, teacher trainers, instructional media center staff, and publishers. It is the "sharing" and "pooling" aspects of task analyses which prompted this discussion of visual layout.

Rationale for Task Analysis (A Summary Statement)

1. In our zeal to help children learn, we must never overlook or downgrade the obvious—*they need good teaching.*

2. Central to good teaching is the teacher's ability to: (a) select an appropriate aim, (b) break the task down into its sequential segments and (c) make necessary individual modifications.

3. Too much emphasis on a search for innovations, on socio-economic and psychological factors and indeed upon the child himself can often lead the teacher away from the key questions: *What is it that I am trying to teach this child?* and *What are the requirements of the task?* (Note: "Requirements of the task" and "sequence of the task" are virtually synonomous. If a specific task is analyzed and a certain number of sequentialized steps emerge, clearly step one is a requirement for step two which in turn becomes a requirement for step three, etc.).

A consideration of task analysis does not in any way preclude other educational goals such as development of attitudes and appreciations, establishing rapport, emotional considerations and social growth. What it *does* effect is a redirection of the teacher's efforts toward the actual teaching process. The effective teacher must learn to think along these lines: "I know how to play checkers. Can I teach this child to play checkers? If so, what is the best way to do it?"

USING CUES

Definition and Purpose

The overall purpose of cues is to enhance the likelihood of the pupil's correct response. A cue may be in the form of a *hint* (or a *prompt)* which facilitates the occurence of the correct response in a precise, limited, circumscribed instance: cuing may also take the form of *modeling* in which a total behavior (and not each approximation leading up to it) is learned—a notable example being the acquisition of language by the child as he observes parent and teacher models (Meacham and Wiesen, 1970, 80-89). The latter aspect has obvious import to the teacher in terms of effecting the emergence of the child's attitudes, values, manners, bearing, etc; it is the hints and prompts aspects of cues,* however, which are directly concerned with the *how* of teaching, relating to the specific pedagogical skills which promote recall.

When a child has difficulty remembering—and this includes the memory of facts (When did Columbus discover America?), systems (reading notes on the musical scale), visual recognition and discrimination (telling the difference between *b* and *d*), words (an expressive aphasic has the word "on the tip of my tongue"), etc.—he can often be helped if we provide him with cues. Cues offer the child a strategy for assisting recall. The process of cuing is an extension of the principle of starting with the known in order to get to the unknown. For example, young children are usually much more conversant, familiar, and comfortable with colors (the known) than with phonics (the unknown). *Words in color* is a method of teaching reading in which "phonetic awareness is exalted . . . through color cues . . ." (Gattegno and Hinman, 1966, 186). All of us have heard the story of the drill sergeant who had to carry a few pebbles in his right hand to help him with directional recall! We can assume that he actually knew his

* Psychologists often use the term "cue" to denote the original stimulus for a desired response. In this respect, the teacher's question is the stimulus (or cue), the child's answer, the response. The written or spoken algorism "6 + 5" is the cue to the child's response "eleven". However, the bond between stimulus and response is often strengthened by some link (a clue, a hint) which will enhance the probability of the stimulus' eliciting the appropriate response. For example, the stimulus question "What is the sound of the short *o*?" can be linked to the response "ah" by remembering that the mouth is rounded—*like the o*—when saying "ah". This link is also correctly called a cue. It is the linking connotation of "cue" which is used in this book.

left from his right, but under the pressure of time (which certainly is the case during close order drill), the sergeant could not differentiate the directions quickly enough and was therefore subject to embarrassing error. Let us analyze his strategy. Whenever he commands a right-turn marching maneuver, he no longer has to think about which is his right—he merely has to think of the pebbles. By developing a strong "pebbles-right" association, the converse association is also formed and strengthened ("I am sure my right hand has the pebbles; therefore my left is the empty one."). If, for some reason, the sergeant still had difficulty remembering in which hand to put the pebbles, he might strengthen the bond by remembering the word "rebels", a clue-word composed of an element from each of the key words *"right"* and *"pebbles"*.

Examples of Cues

Mnemonic devices are sometimes quite effective. Some of them are well-known:

The musical scale can be cued by *E*VERY *G*OOD *B*OY *D*OES *F*INE and F-A-C-E for the treble clef's lines and spaces; *G*REAT *B*RITAIN *D*ID *F*IGHT *A*MERICA and *A* *C*OW *E*ATS *G*RASS for the bass clef's lines and spaces.

The Indian Chief named Soh-Cah-Toa is the clue for the trigonometric functions:

$$\textit{s}\text{ine}=\frac{\text{side }\textit{o}\text{pposite}}{\textit{h}\text{ypotenuse}},\ \textit{c}\text{osine}=\frac{\text{side }\textit{a}\text{djacent}}{\textit{h}\text{ypotenuse}},\ \textit{t}\text{angent}=\frac{\text{side }\textit{o}\text{pposite}}{\text{side }\textit{a}\text{djacent}}$$

The name S. P. COHN can help one remember the elements of protoplasm: sulphur, phosphorous, carbon, oxygen, hydrogen, and nitrogen.

Rhymes and Songs can also serve as strategies (e.g., "Thirty days hath September . . .", "When two vowels go walking, the first does the talking," the "I can say my A-B-C song").

Words within a word can be used as clues. For example, the difference between "peace" and "piece" can be recalled with the aid of "a piece of pie"; remembering that the principal is your "pal" can help the child use "principal" and "principle" correctly.

The differentiation between "what" and "want" can be clued by pointing out the word "hat" in "what". This association can become fixed if the teacher tells the child this "story": "A boy had many hats. (Draw pictures of 4 or 5 hats, or use actual hats.) His mother said, 'You may go out, but don't forget to wear your hat.' The boy asked, 'What hat?' " This story should be exaggerated with gestures, expressions, etc. The child begins to associate "hat" with "what." If the word in question contains "hat," it must be "what"; therefore, if it looks something like "what" but doesn't contain "hat," it must be "want."

Cognitive cues abound in the area of arithmetic relationships:

Children who have difficulty adding examples like $7 + 8$, $6 + 5$, $9 + 8$, etc., are often helped with the strategy of "doubles and near doubles":

6	6
+6	+7

8	8
+8	+7

Learning to multiply 5's generally precedes multiplying by 6 (not because 5 comes before 6, but because of our base 10 system: nickels and dimes; games in which we count by 5's; the fact that multiples of 5's have only two possible endings—5 or 0). Therefore, the example 7×6 can be approached as 7×5 plus 7×1.

It is easier to add a number to ten than to nine. Therefore, we can teach $9 + \square$ via "closing the ten", i.e., when *given* $9 + 6$, *think* $9 + 1 = 10$, $10 + 5 = 15$.

Another example of a cognitive clue is the use of context to promote recall of a specific word. A child may confuse "horse" with "house" when reading them as isolated words. By presenting the word in a printed sentence, (e.g., "Jack will ride my horse."), a context clue emerges, enhancing the probability of a correct response.

Still another illustration of cognitive cues is the knowledge of word composition. A child may be guided towards comprehending a "new" word via a study of prefixes, suffixes, and roots.

Combining two words to form a third can be useful at times. For example, if a student is trying to remember that blood spurts out of a cut artery but flows from a severed vein, the word "sparta", combining *spurt* with *artery* can assist recall.

Word derivatives can be effective clues. Foreign language vocabulary memory (a paired-associate task), can often be facilitated by providing such links:

French	*Link*	*English*
main	(manufacture)	hand
donner	(donation)	give
froid	(freeze)	cold

Gagné (1970, 137-138), suggests an alternate instructional method of requiring the pupil to create his own link (any word, image or thought which will join the stimulus and response words).

Visual associations are often useful. The area of penmanship is replete with such possibilities:

The written *z* can be clued by the number *3*.

The written *d* can be clued by: Think of a *C*. Now start the *C* from the bottom. *C* Then finish the *d*."

The child can use the printed *S* to help him remember how to write the numeral *8*.

The numeral *4* has four points: 4 ; the numeral *3* has three points: 3

The joining element of the written H can be taught in the following manner: "Draw these two lines: 9/ . Now rotate the paper, so that they become the ruled lines of writing paper . Now simply write the letter l .

Rotate the paper back to its original position: H .

b and *d* confusion can often be cleared up by pointing out to the child that the capital printed B actually contains the small b: B . The strategy, then, enfolds this way: Whenever you see a letter like *b* or *d*, "put a little half circle on top on the same side of the line". Now ask yourself, "Is that a 'good (proper) B'?" If so, then the original letter was a *b*; if not, it was a *d*. (Note: At first, the child may actually have to draw the half circle; later he can trace it with his finger; finally, he simply imagines it drawn.)

The clock has always been a favorite cue, from the visual association standpoint as well as cognitively. Mechanics, engineers, and scientists are often aided in learning, performing, and communicating items involving movement directionality by referring to the concepts of "clockwise" and "counter-clockwise". The face of the clock offers additional directional (but stationary) clues: "twelve o'clock high", "two o'clock position", etc. Spalding (1957, 74) utilized the clock's face in the instruction of penmanship, stressing particularly the ten, two, eight, and four o'clock positions: e.g., the letter 'C' starts at two o'clock and proceeds counter-clockwise to four o'clock; 's' starts at two o'clock, moves to ten o'clock, cuts across the face of the clock to four o'clock, and from there proceeds to eight o'clock.

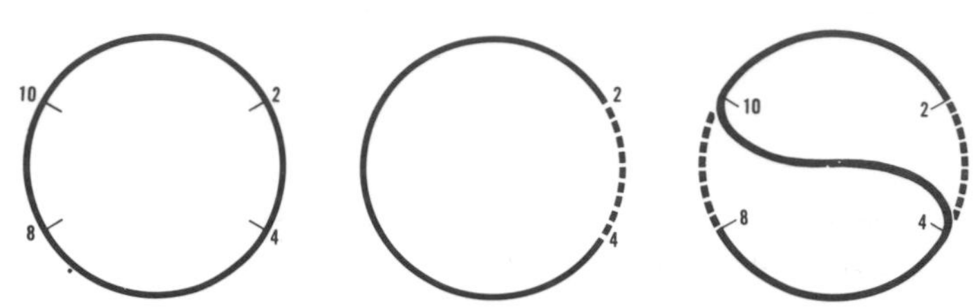

Teachers of reading have often complained that there is no relationship between the letter's shape and its sound. This is basically correct; however, with a little imagination, some cues can be offered. For example, the letter "S" looks like a snake—and a snake's hiss sound like the "S". The letter "h" can be seen to resemble a chair—when we're tired, we sit in a chair and our tired panting sounds like the "h".

Structural Reading (Stern and Gould, 1965, 159) deliberately creates key pictures, imposing the letters upon the picture.
(See page 103).

Additional Purposes of Cues

Although the concept of cuing as an aid to memory has been stressed, there seem to be at least two other purposes involved in cuing:

1. Problem-solving strategies (i.e., creative thinking) can be nurtured through cues. If one wishes to teach a child to solve a puzzle (e.g., present the pupil with a number of wooden matches arranged in a set of squares and ask him to re-arrange a given number of matches, thereby altering the original amount of squares,) the most effective cue is not to do the puzzle for him, not to verbalize the strategy, but to illustrate several similar puzzles (and their solutions), and allow the child to make the discovery

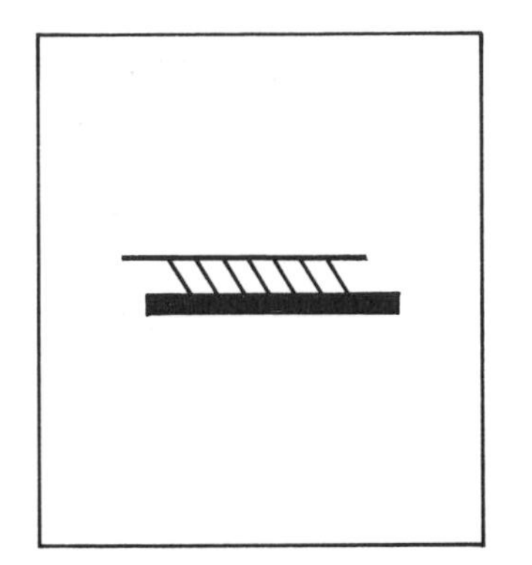

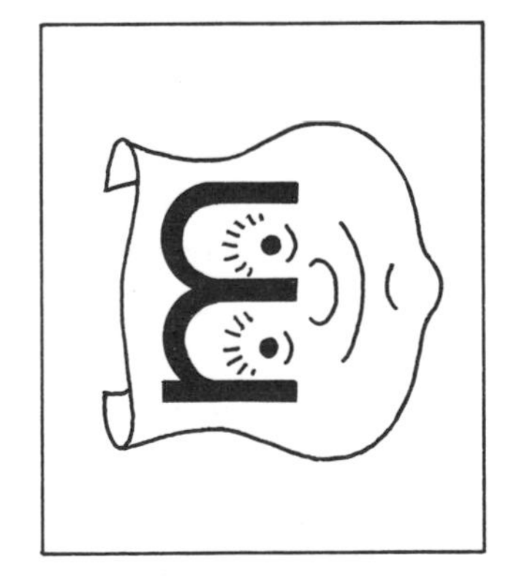

of the strategy (the principles and rules), for himself (Gagné, 1970, 217-219).

2. Cuing is also related to attention. Selecting cues which are relevant, decreasing extraneous stimuli which may act as false cues, providing numerous cues and accentuating them (colors, arrows, marks, underlines, etc.), can all serve to focus the child's attention on the task at hand (Meacham and Wiesen, 1970).

Criteria for Effective Cues

Some criteria for the effective employing of cues can be stated:

1. The clue or cue must always be easier than the final task. In the penmanship examples one sees that: *3* is indeed easier to write than *z*, tracing a *C* starting from the bottom is easier than writing the *d* for most children, rotating the paper and writing *l* is easier than trying to remember how to join the written *H's* two parallel lines. Many children who have reversal problems with *b* and *d* never reverse the *B*. The ABC song is easier to memorize than are the "lyrics" alone. The word "hat" presents less reading problems than the word "what", etc.

2. The "performance" (i.e., understanding, ability to deal with, etc.), of the cues must be within the child's repetoire. If the child not only reverses b and d but also reverses the capital B (the cue), as well, then he cannot use the B as a cue. The teacher must either actually *teach* him how to *perform* the cue or discover some other strategy within his repetoire.

3. The cues must not be too vague.

4. The cues should not serve as distracting elements. (The child must be observed closely to see if the cue is a help or a hindrance.)

5. Cues, being in reality crutches, should be gradually phased out. (There is an art in knowing how and when to do this. Again, intense experience with one child at a time can be of invaluable aid to the teacher.)

USING REPETITION

Objections

Of all the methods, approaches, techniques, modifications (call it what you will) known to education, the one process which, without a doubt, has been maligned the most is that of repetition. There are many reasons for this. To begin with, repetition has a strong punitive connotation ("Write 'I must not talk' three hundred times," "Do it over till you get it right," etc.) Another reason for its lack of popularity as an instructional technique is that it conjures up such negative images as "plodding along" and "grinding out," denoting dullness rather than enthusiasm, sameness rather than variety, boredom rather than inspiration. Then, too, repetition is thought of as being related to a narrow, limited, fragmented goal rather than to a broad and meaningful purpose. It also smacks of "training" (in the derogatory connotation of this term—such as an animal trainer), the feeling being that the trainer is imposing his will upon the passive, and often unwilling trainee. After all, those high stepping horses certainly did not ask to be trained! Repetition as a teaching experience is often shunned since it can produce a performer who has no understanding of the meaning of his performance: e.g., to be trained to "count" from one to ten orally, but with no idea of the concept of one-to-one correspondence; to be able to recite the "Pledge of Allegiance" without grasping its meaning (in ignorance of the definition of and therefore, mispronouncing—much of its vocabulary); reading by rote; etc. Criticism of this kind of rote performance reached its height in Charlie Chaplin's "Modern Times", which caricatured the dehumanizing aspect and the sheer monotony associated with our industrial assembly-line production system.

Among the exceptional population, repetition is said to apply most to the mentally retarded group, the stereotype being a dull individual who "isn't ever going to get anyplace" painstakingly practicing some low-level, almost inconsequential skill over and over and over again. Brain-injured children frequently perseverate —that is, needlessly repeat in action (e.g., making a toy's wheels go around and around unceasingly; continuing to "crayon in" an outlined box furiously and erratically, ignoring its borders) and in word (talking incessantly; fixating on a particular topic; asking an inordinate amount of questions—often the same ones). By far, the severest objection to the process of repetition as an educational technique is that it seems to be utterly devoid of any creativity—from either the teaching or learning standpoints.

Using Repetition Productively

Despite the validity of the above criticisms, repetition as a teaching method should be examined closely to see if any possible merit can accrue from it under any circumstances. It may turn out that, like fire, it can be either very beneficial or very harmful depending upon the conditions surrounding its use. A key consideration would be the intent of the teacher: Does he assign drill work punitively? If so, it will be perceived by the child as such and will indeed be punishing. Does he assign the same material to the child repeatedly because he expects that the child will *never* be ready for more advanced work? If so, it will become a self-fulfilling prophecy. Does he use the same kind and amount of drill and repetition even after the child has learned the lesson? If so, it will, at the least, be wasted time and will very likely contribute to the child's negativism and lack of motivation. Is it used for prolonged periods of time, frequently beyond the point of fatigue? If so, the child will associate the teaching-learning process with unpleasant feelings and, again, negativism and hostility can result.

If the teacher's intent, on the other hand, is to help the pupil (educationally, psychologically, and motivationally), and if the teacher is trained and sophisticated pedagogically as well as in child development, then repetition need not be avoided "like the plague." In fact, the teacher who uses this instructional method judiciously and selectively may find that it reaps large rewards. Some of the benefits deriving from the use of repetition are:

Increased competency. Training, per se, can have either positive or negative valence for the trainee. If one is coerced into training, the harmful results may far outweigh any gains. On the other hand, if one desires to develop a skill and embraces the training, then advantages accrue. For an aspiring and somewhat potentially talented singer, the adage "practice makes perfect" is well-taken. Coaching, of course, is needed, but the major portion of the neophyte's efforts will be devoted to sheer drill. Via this repetition, the correct vocal techniques are developed, mastered and maintained; at the same time, incorrect practices—since the feedback (listening to oneself sing) is negative—will be extinguished. The concept of "habit" is a valid one here. If an automobile driver had to think about each driving maneuver before he executed it, an erratic, hesitating driving style would emerge. But through practice, correct driving *habits* are generated resulting in a more competent driver and a smoother ride. Similarly, training in multiplication tables can lead to the *habit* of giving the correct answers.

Diminished cue time. One of the criticisms of providing cues to facilitate learning is that the cue becomes a crutch. The most powerful method of entirely eliminating or at least drastically diminishing the need for cues can be summed up in one word—

practice. Suppose, for example, a child is trying to learn to count by two's, the goal being the ability to say "two, four, six, eight, . . . etc." quickly and accurately. The teacher has provided the following explanation which will serve as the child's cue: "Look at the original number; *think of,* but do not say, the next number; now *say* the number after that." Fine. The child has a general understanding of the system and can produce the proper response, though not too quickly: He sees the number six. "Now let's see. I have to think of the next number". (pause) "Now what is the next number?" (pause) "Oh, yes, it's seven. Now what do I do—*think* it or *say* it?" (pause) "Yes, I remember. I *think* it. Now what do I do?" (pause) "I have to find the number after that. I believe it's eight. Now let me see. I *thought* the number seven, so I'll *say* eight. There! That's the answer. Eight."

With many practice periods, all of this thinking is compressed. The child goes through the entire process each time, but faster and faster. The very speed of the process eliminates possible errors. For example, if the child thinks of "seven" quickly, he doesn't have to ask himself "Now did I *think* of seven or did I *say* seven." He remembers because it happened just a fraction of a second ago. Whether or not one ever discards a crutch completely is a moot point. Through practice, one learns to go through the "stimulus-cue-response" process quicker and quicker so that the net result is either the actual elimination of the need for the cue, or the ability to perform *as if* the cue were dropped.

Provision for consolidation. A teacher may develop considerable skill in creating—or selecting—an instructional sequence, the aim of which is totally suitable for the child, (i.e., in consonance with his age, readiness level, grade, needs, interest, etc.) and still the child may fail to learn. One reason for this failure might be the teacher's neglecting to consolidate the child's learning at each of the sequentialized steps of the task analysis. That is to say, it is not enough merely to "cover" an instructional step before proceeding to the next one. Assuming that the prior step is preparatory to the one following it, then simply exploring this preparatory step, talking about it, exposing the child to it, etc., is insufficient. What is needed is a thorough mastery. Consolidating denotes stopping, reviewing, taking inventory, collating, summarizing, and, in the vernacular "putting it all together" so that mastery does indeed occur.

According to Ausubel (1966, 237), an optimal learning environment—especially helpful in educating the culturally disadvantaged—entails the consolidating of current learning tasks prior to the introduction of new ones, thereby providing the base for successful sequential learning while reciprocally militating against any "unreadiness" for the next sequential steps. He further states (238-239) that overlearning makes possible the transfer of past learnings to new learning tasks, and that overlearning, in turn, is dependent upon:

1. a sufficient number of spaced repetitions and review;
2. adequate "intra-task repetitiveness" (i.e., repetition at a given step in a basic way should occur before going on to any ". . . intra- or inter-task diversification";) and
3. selected practice periods on only the difficult elements of a particular step of a sequence, rather than upon that entire step.

Teachers, when using textbooks and workbooks with mentally retarded children, will undoubtedly attest to the need for this consolidation (i.e., repetition). Such books, even the ones prepared especially for these slower learners, virtually cry out for consolidation at each page. The fact that the child has "completed" the material on one page does not in any way guarantee that he will be ready for the next. In almost every case, he will not be able to do so without the consolidation, mastery, overlearning, "clinching," that only repetition can produce. (Note: repetition, here, most emphatically does not mean "doing" that very page over and over again. What it does mean is that the same material, topic, idea, concept, etc., should be repetitively presented, *but in a variety of ways,* so that what results is a set of parallel activities, each differing from the others in form, but having identical content and goal.)

Isn't it interesting that the topic of consolidating (and mastery) as discussed here blends the traditional, "old-fashioned" ideas of repetition with the current, scientific, almost innovative approach of educational task analysis?

Improved self-confidence. Very often, children who catch on to a "little piece" of the learning task but not all of it, become anxious, frustrated, and harbor feelings of self-deprecation. This tension and self-doubt render their performance even poorer, and hence a negative spiral is generated. Overlearning—via repetition—can break this cycle. By practicing the same material repeatedly, the child "knows that he knows," sees himself as a learner rather than as a failure, is less tense, and views school and the learning situation positively. Moreover, others see him performing adequately and he gains their respect rather than the previous castigation. The quality of the child's performance improves even more. In brief, a cycle still exists, but the direction has been completely reversed.

Many emotionally disturbed children cannot tolerate failure. "Success-assured" activities are recommended for them initially so that they might gain in feelings of self-confidence. The nature of these activities is largely repetitive, the aim being not to teach the child any new subject matter, but just to show him that he can perform successfully.

Heightened structure. Children frequently need considerable structure in their learning environment. Excessive stimuli, inconsistency, an overly-permissive atmosphere and too many choices can prove chaotic. This is particularly true in the case of the minimally brain-injured, who often are distractible, hyperactive, impulsive, and perseverative. Just as there are some minimally brain damaged who may not require excessive structuring, there are many other children—handicapped as well as "normal"—who would benefit from structuring.

Barry (1961, 21) set forth a precise and extremely clear, well-written definition of structure:

> We mean putting things in order, we mean teaching limits and sequence, we mean clarifying, dramatizing, simplifying, concretizing. We mean bringing the foreground sharply into focus, blocking out non-essentials. We mean touching, and feeling, and looking, and listening, outlining, and underlining. We mean performing a simple activity in deliberate, sequential steps, in response to deliberate, sequential commands such as, "Pick it up, look at it, where does it go?, put it there." We mean every technique, device, or trick that will help the child to hear, to see, to understand—to take meaning out of chaos—for until we structure the world for some of these children, it is just that—chaos.

Repetition can very well be subsumed under Barry's definition of structure. "Clarifying", "simplifying", "concretizing", all denote repetition. So does "touching, and feeling, and looking, and listening, outlining and underlining", in that the same instructional frame may be repeated in all of these different ways. Additional elements of structure would be reinforcement, consistency, review—all implying some kind of repetition.

Repetition and Variety

At first glance, the adjectives "repetitive" and "varied" seem to be opposites. This need not be so. In fact, effective teaching frequently demands repetition but in a variety of ways. This is not at all an exercise in semantics. A pupil may be at a certain level, not yet ready to go ahead. How can we help him to consolidate his prior learnings so that he will be able to go on to the next step? By repetition! But does this mean doing the same arithmetic examples over and over again in the same way? Definitely not! A child can be taught that five plus four are nine in many different ways. He can try to discover the sum by looking at the two groups of objects, by feeling them with or without looking at them and/or by listening to them (the teacher instructs the child to look away but to count each book as the teacher places it—loudly—on the desk)—the well-known multisensory approach. He can use a variety of objects (pennies, cubes of sugar, discs, tongue depressors, pencils, desks, etc.). Pictures, drawings, dots or lines can be employed representationally. The child might initially be encouraged to count on his fingers.

The algorism can be presented differently:

$$\begin{array}{r} 5 \\ +4 \\ \hline \end{array} \qquad 5 + 4 = \square \qquad \text{five} + 4 = ?$$

The algorism can be combined with visual representation:

$$\boxed{5} + \boxed{\cdot\cdot\cdot\cdot} = \square$$

Money can be used:

A "ten's frame" (a string of ten beads—five red and five green—strung onto a cardboard mounting) can be helpful in having the child see that five and four are "almost ten". Arithmetic programs and kits which use different size rods to depict the different numbers one to ten (Cuisenaire rods; Stern's Structured Arithmetic) are yet another approach: By putting the "five-rod" and "four-rod" together, the child can again see many relationships: "It is almost ten," "It is way more than two or three," "Five and four together are more than either by itself," etc.

The alert teacher can integrate content into functional experiences: preparation for trips, planning for parties, games, arts and crafts (e.g., measuring with a ruler), taking attendance, distributing materials—all of these provide additional opportunity to experience "five plus four."

It can—and should—be approached cognitively in a variety of ways:

1. counting five objects, and then four objects, starting at one;
2. starting with the five objects, and adding four more, counting by ones (i.e., "six-seven-eight-nine");
3. starting with five objects, and adding four more, counting by twos (i.e., "five-seven-nine"); and
4. begin with the known, five plus five, and seeing five plus four as "one less".

It is virtually axiomatic that writing reinforces reading. Therefore a child who is learning to read should experience writing simultaneously for best results. If the child finds reading difficult, he may need considerable writing reinforcement. But the fact that he has only a meager sight vocabulary drastically limits the number of different words he should be assigned in written activities. Does this mean that a great deal of repetition is necessary? Yes. But does it also mean that he must write the same words over and over again and be assigned the identical written exercise each time? Most assuredly not! The same words can be written in a variety of exercises:

1. Suppose it is advantageous for a beginning reader to write sentences such as "My house is big," "Come and play," "Look and see my puppy" many times. Instead of having him write the same sentence ten times, the teacher should

designate three copies of each sentence as an assignment; then repeat the assignment on succeeding days.

2. A variation of the above suggestion can be for the teacher to write the model sentence at the top of a page in the child's notebook. Then write the sentence ten more times under the model, but each time omitting one or more words—or even parts of a word—making sure to leave a space for each omission, thus visually cuing the child to the fact of the omissions. The child's assignment is to complete each sentence, referring to the model.

3. The teacher can write several sentences on a page, each one in scrambled order. The child, in the space provided under each of the teacher's sentences, will unscramble them.

4. Many words lend themselves to workbook-type activities. For example, instead of simply having the child write the words "big" and "little" many times in rows, the teacher may have an exercise like this:

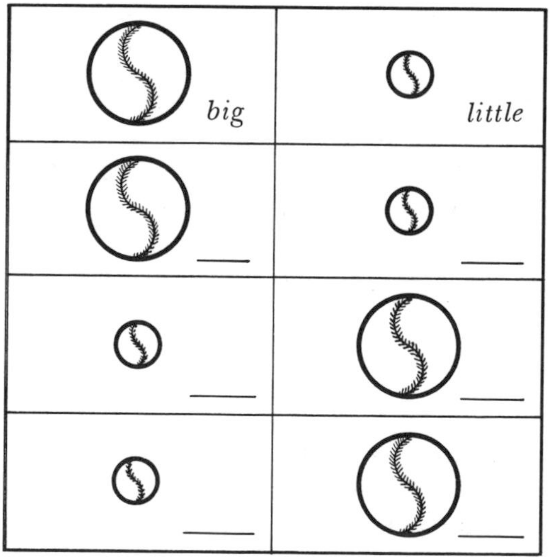

big	*little*
___	___
___	___
___	___

Similar written exercises can easily be prepared for words such as "in-on," "one-two-three," "up-down," "red-blue," etc.

Studying Spelling is almost pure repetition. Mastery is often achieved by repeated writing until one gets the "feel" of a word and has seen it so many times that he can tell when it "looks" wrong or right. This method of studying Spelling, though, is applicable for more mature, capable students. Children who find Spelling difficult should be taught in a variety of ways: *Visually* (looking at the word); *Auditorially* (saying the word and spelling it aloud); *Tactually* (feeling a sandpaper cut-out of the word and "writing" the word with index finger on the desk); and *Kinesthetically* ("writing" the word in the air; having the teacher "write" the word on the child's wrist or back, the teacher's index finger simulating the pencil.) There is a cognitive approach to Spelling as well—Spelling rules, phonics, a consideration of the difficult parts of the words, a studying of prefixes and suffixes, etc. In addition, a variety of written materials can be helpful—crayon, chalk, pencil, pen, paintbrush, writing in sand, using a stylus (a sharpened stick) to write in a pan of clay, finger-paint, etc.

Only in rare instances, when there is considerable talent and high motivation can repetition *in the same way* be helpful: Cramming for tests at the college level often involves summarizing the written notes, then copying them over and over again, omitting at each trial those portions which the student feels he knows. In this way, repetition facilitates memory. It has been pointed out (Gagné, 1970, 151-152) that many excellent speakers, having developed a flair for and an interest in oration at an early age, memorized passages from Shakespeare, the Bible, or historical speeches. They memorized via repetition, and the fruits of the repetitive processs increased their self-confidence, oratory style, and vocabulary. These instances, obviously, are exceptions. In general, repetition is helpful only if presented in a variety of ways.

The practice of varying activities—even within the same sequential step and entailing the same contents—is a definite asset in promoting attention. Further requirements, in addition to the stipulation of variety, are that each of the activities should be relatively brief in duration, and that activities requiring physical movement be included.

Criteria for Effective Use of Repetition

For repetition to be used as an effective instructional technique, the following criteria should be observed:

1. A given instructional frame should be repeated, but in a variety of ways.
2. The practice should be distributed, spaced over a period of time rather than massed.
3. If fatigue sets in, it is obviously time to change the activity or the topic.
4. Great consideration should be given to how the child *perceives* the repetition. (Does he think it punitive? Does it "prove" to him that he is dull, etc.?)
5. Motivation is a key factor. It is essential that the child enter into the repetitive process of instruction with a positive attitude. For example, Riessman (1962, 84) presents a case in which a seemingly deadly repetitive mode of instruction was used advantageously. A teacher of a disadvantaged class used the technique of asking *each* child in the class the same question ("What is six plus eight?"), whether or not the first child answered correctly. According to the teacher, this technique insured that the children stayed awake. He used a sort of game approach by having the children primed to see how many would get it right and how many would miss. Clearly, as Riess-

man was quick to point out, this activity should not be used indefinitely since, among other things, it is time-consuming. Initially, however, it was advantageous in developing the auditory attention of these children. Later other approaches were substituted.

In summary, then, repetition as an instructional technique has been greatly misunderstood and underrated. Far from precluding creativity, one should, in fact strive to develop *creative repetition.*

"WRONG-NESS" REVISITED

Flexibility is an important aspect of instruction. The truly effective teacher is open-minded, rather than dogmatic in approach. A willingness to "bend" precedes the ability to do so. And both are born of self-confidence. To put it differently, the teacher who is "good" and knows that he is "good" often develops the art (and attitude) of considering, examining and re-examining, restructuring, and occasionally shifting beliefs when warranted. (At least he can *afford*—from a psychological standpoint—to do so.) He adopts an "I can be persuaded" style—contemplative but at the same time dynamic and questioning. He is willing to subject his own values and philosophies to scrutiny, is not defensive about appearing consistent at all costs, and is not at all impressed with the inertial arguments (e.g., "But we've always done it that way.", "But everyone knows that that's wrong.") frequently used to justify a particular instructional method or goal.

An excellent application of this flexibility is to take a hard look at some of the commonly espoused "rights" and "wrongs" in the teaching-learning process. The entire area of "wrong-ness" can be revisited from three points of view:

1. understanding the child's "wrong" answer,
2. using the child's weakness (that is, "wrong" behavior) to advantage, and

3. considering the feasibility of deliberately employing "wrong" methods.

Understanding the Child's "Wrong" Answers

A great deal of the instructional process is devoted to questioning and answering. The teacher poses the question; the child answers. This is done orally as well as in writing. The answer is evaluated and some judgment rendered. The judgment can be in the form of a test score, homework grade, a simple "yes" or "no," or some subtle teacher mannerism registering either pleasure or displeasure. It is well known that all learning entails failure, but that failure, certainly when excessive, can be ego-deflating. Therefore, a laudable goal would be to keep failure experiences at a minimum. One way of achieving this is to make sure that the child's response is not deemed wrong, when with some consideration and empathic thinking it may be seen to possess many "right" elements. This is an extremely important concept since if the child's response and thought processes leading up to the response are really correct and they go unrewarded, this in itself is harmful. It literally adds insult to injury if, in addition, we label him "wrong."

Suppose a pupil, upon seeing the word "invaluable," understands it to mean "worthless." Now, stripped to the essentials, the fact of the matter is that the answer is wrong. However, doesn't the child deserve considerable credit for applying his knowledge of the prefix's meaning, linking it with the root word, and deriving a definition? Instead of gravely pronouncing, "No, that's wrong," the teacher might explain to the child that this is "one of those exceptions," that "invaluable" (implying of such value that it is impossible to place a price tag on it) actually is more valuable than "valuable", but that the child's reasoning was quite valid.

Other sources of error can derive from an overly concrete style of thinking. Van Witsen (1967, 7-8) tells of a child who, upon being instructed to punch a hole in a piece of paper, might punch out the hole with a hole puncher correctly but then deliberately punch a hole with his fist as well!

Applying rules of grammar which obtain in regular cases to irregular cases can account for other errors. If a child—usually one from a disadvantaged area—says, "I 'run-ed' to school," the net result is wrong, but his logic is correct.

Homonyms and/or phrases that sound alike can be other sources of error. "The cross I bear" can register as "the cross-eye (d) bear"! The critical teacher will endeavor to understand the manner and limitations of the child's perceptual (auditory as well as visual) repetoire.

A child's background, if different from those of his teachers and publishers of educational material, can lead to erroneous responses. For example, a picture of a doorman might be perceived as a policeman or a fireman. A picture of a log might be interpreted as a rolled-up carpet.

The teacher must develop sensitivity to the child in two ways: he learns to follow the child's train of thought (and this implies an in-depth knowledge of the child—his style, his background, his idiosyncrasies, and he becomes aware of the child's ego needs. By letting the child know that he understands what led him to his particular response, the teacher is in effect telling him, "You're important—so much so that I am learning about you and I want to learn even more about you. I understand how you 'thought out' that one. You really are quite a good thinker." All of this, of course, takes the sting out of the wrong answer. The child will probably be relaxed, less stubbornly defensive, and will consequently be more ready to accept and understand the reasoning accompanying the "right" answer.

A distinction, of course, should be made here between answers which are totally wrong (say, a wild guess, a completely incorrect concept, one hundred per cent forgetfulness, etc.) and those which only seem wrong. Even the former should be handled tactfully, but it is important that the child learn to differentiate between a correct and an incorrect response, lest he develop an "anything goes" value system.

Using the Child's Weaknesses to Advantage

One frequently diagnoses a child educationally and/or psychologically and comes up with a profile of strengths and weaknesses. Some of the weaknesses are difficult to "cure." Yet they are there, they are part of the child. Perhaps with time, patience, various therapies, and maturity, they can be ameliorated. But his education can't wait! How can one teach him and, at the same time, reckon with these weaknesses?

Fortunately, as one gets to know the child, it may be possible to turn a weakness into an advantage. This is not to say that the weakness is actually desirable. If given a choice, one would of course like the deficit minimized. What one actually does is to understand the child, take him "where he is at," and teach him. Some examples of negative traits which might be used to advantage are:

Hyperactivity: A child has a lot of energy. He can't seem to sit still. He is always on the go. If one attempts to make him sit still and conform just as though the problem were non-existent, the likelihood is that frustrations and emotional problems will result (at least for the child and probably for the teacher as well!). What is recommended here has often been said before: Let the child use up his energies in worthwhile activities. Channel his efforts and physical movements in constructive ways. Let him help in distributing, collecting and storing of materials. If he is given to pounding, let him play the drums. If he tears things up, let him make paper maché. Gym and shop periods are helpful; similarly, creative expression, dramatics, and music can prove useful.

Perseveration: This is a behavioral trait which is typical of many minimally brain-damaged children, but is by no means their exclusive province. It involves doing the same thing over and over again, well beyond the point of completion in a driven, erratic manner. An oversimplified yet somewhat valid explanation is to point out that there is a value judgment denoted here: If the child is doing something over and over again *and we like it,* it is called perseverance; if we *don't* like it, it is called perseveration. At any rate, perseveration (besides denoting neuroticism, drivenness, rigidity, etc.) still implies a capacity to stick with it. The classroom teacher should at times seek to provide the perseverative child with tasks requiring little shifting and make these as free from distractions as possible. The child's perseveration (i.e., inability to shift readily from one situation to another) can thus be used to advantage, depending upon the teacher's task selection.

Distractibility: Many children are unable to pay attention to the task at hand but are easily sidetracked by background sensory data. The teacher must ask himself: "Are there times when it would redound to the child's advantage to be distracted away from the task at hand?" Of course there are! Suppose the "task at hand" is a temper tantrum, a depressed mood, or a non-productive "fooling around" activity. The teacher, knowing that the child is distractible, can at times lead him away from this negativism with relative ease. Show him a picture; teach him a trick; tell him a brief story; begin playing a game. In short, change the subject.

In addition to these specific examples, there are other broad categories in which the teacher might endeavor to utilize a child's weakness to advantage. The need for attention and recognition can lead a child into unwholesome, counter-productive, often anti-social behavior; yet this very need can be utilized positively as the teacher steers the child's behavior into more socially acceptable channels. Similarly, a child's curiosity may take the form of "noseyness" and prove offensive to others, thereby engendering feelings of hostility towards him. This identical trait of curiosity, however, can be molded, nurtured, and modified so that it stimulates learning and actually leads to a more interesting personality. Many of the traits of the disadvantaged were originally considered to be weaknesses (e.g., a slow, "mulling over" style; motoric rather than verbal preferences; the ability to express anger). However, it has been pointed out that these very traits are often "hidden positives." Seen in this light, the teacher might very well begin to use them to the child's advantage.

Deliberately Employing "Wrong" Instructional Techniques

There is a considerable amount of prejudgment which goes on in education regarding methodology. At times, teachers, on the scantest of evidence, or on the basis of vaguely having recalled someone espouse an opinion, or possibly by virtue of intuition (and it need not necessarily be a passionate belief), or simply by force of habit, firm up their own methodology system, sharply differentiating "right" techniques from "wrong" ones. The truly creative teacher is one who is not quick to apply the "wrong" or "right" label, but instead looks at each situation (i.e., the individual child, his educational profile, his level of achievement, and his style of learning) and chooses from a large repertoire of techniques and approaches those most likely to help the child learn.

The vast majority of so-called "wrong" techniques which may actually be helpful fall under the broad category of *intermittent techniques.* That is to say, in order to achieve the last sequential step of mastery, a previous step (often a less mature but more concrete one) must itself first be mastered. In fact, successful teachers frequently find it necessary to actually *teach* the less mature approach to the child as a preparatory step towards fulfilling the particular instructional goal in entirety. Some examples follow:

1. Teaching a child to count on his fingers may be an excellent means of promoting the one-to-one correspondence between the stated numeral and the object being counted.
2. Some children learn to read best when taught to point to each word. True, this takes some of the expression out of their oral reading, but it does insure that words are not skipped, that the child correlates what he says with what he sees, and that memorization of a sentence or a paragraph does not substitute for reading. At times, some children who are distractible and impulsive may require a "frame" (an index card in which a slot has been cut out) which, as it is moved across the page, exposes only one word at a time.
3. A marker is a well-known technique to help the child stay on the line.
4. "Adding apples and oranges" can sometimes prove helpful. Consider the following sequence:

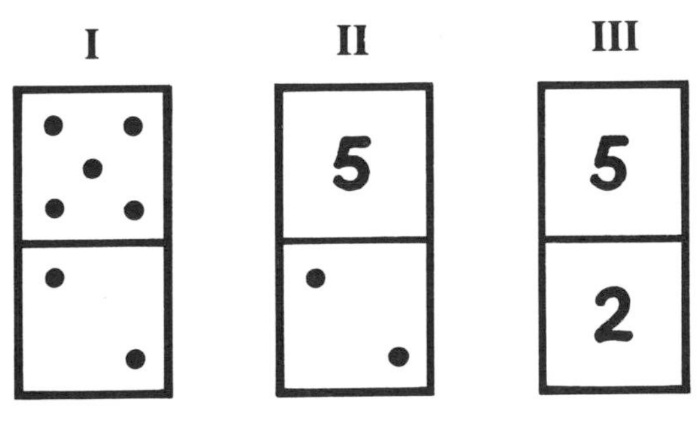

The second algorism seems "wrong" since it mixes the abstract or written numeral with the concrete dots. Yet it is a very important step in moving from the first algorism to the third one, in that it forces more abstract behavior—the child is moved away from immaturely counting all seven dots; he must begin by saying "five" and then simply add the other two dots.

5. Rote reading has been criticized, and rightly so. Nevertheless, it is a start. If a child can read by rote (i.e., read a page correctly but derive very little comprehension from it), the task then is to increase comprehension. By reducing the dosages and the level, and by emphasizing comprehension, one in effect uses the rote reading—for that is the only kind the child knows at this point—to promote non-rote learning. To put it differently, isn't the child who can read but has poor comprehension nevertheless better off than the child who cannot read and who perhaps has poor auditory comprehension as well?

6. The same can be said for rote counting. If the child can recite the numerals one to ten in sequence but can't apply this skill to actually counting objects, at least it represents a tool. This is "where he is at." The effective instructor uses the child's rote counting ability to promote meaningful counting skills.

7. Phonics programs often necessitate instructing the child to exaggerate pronunciation. In a sense, this is wrong. After all, the word isn't "ham-m-m-m-m-m-m-m"; it's simply "ham"! Yet, it is an appropriate procedure to deliberately teach the child to exaggerate the pronunciation in saying and thinking the word, so that he may more easily be able to identify the final consonant.

Other instances in which "wrong" teaching may be purposely employed involve encouraging the child to hang onto *part* of an immature technique in order to prevent the emergence of a tedious and ego-deflating plateau. Suppose Irene is learning cursive writing. She can write *rene* but has a great deal of difficulty with the *I*. The teacher, sensing the ego-building aspect attached to the child's being encouraged to write—not print—her name, might very well encourage her to print the "I," then write the rest:

Irene

A "wrong" technique can sometimes be pegged to a specific medical/psychological need. For example, most children should be taught to print (manuscript) before they learn to write (cursive). Printing uses the same shaped letters which are found in reading. Hence, it does not confuse the child by introducing an alphabet which is different in appearance. Many minimally brain-injured children however do better at writing, because it is more of a continuous kinesthetic experience, eliminating the stop-go pattern of printing.

It is important that the teacher be able to justify his choice of "wrong teaching methods. For instance, he may methodically opt to allow grammatical errors to stand—at least temporarily—in a child's creative writing; too much correction might stifle creativity and lead to stereotyped performance. Another example is the case of a teacher's specifically instructing the child *not* to use complete sentences. Suppose one asks the child, "How much is three and four?" The quickest response would be simply "Seven." The repetition by the child of, "Three and four is . . .", while utilizing a complete sentence, may be tantamount to stalling, allowing him additional time to arrive at the answer. Besides this case, teachers in general may at times wish their pupils to answer in incomplete sentences, since this is how we ordinarily speak in conversation.

In a sense, anytime one provides the child with a clue (e.g., "*i* before *e* except after *c*"; "when two vowels go walking, the first does the talking"; when adding nine and six, "close the tens"—that is—think, "Nine plus one equals ten, then ten plus five equals fifteen"; the small *b* is contained in the capital *B*), it can be considered "wrong" since we are teaching the child an *intermediate* step or strategy. In fact, weaning is the final step of cuing.

The master teacher, then, is one who learns to evaluate—and appreciate—the child's "wrong" answers, and who can deal with "wrong" traits, (i.e., use the child's weaknesses to advantage) and who knows when and how to employ "wrong" methods. All of these clearly demand a thorough knowledge of the child. The one-to-one instructional setting offers optimal training in the ability to observe children, interpret their needs, and come forth with the appropriate, *individualized* instructional techniques.

FOSTERING INDEPENDENCE

It is entirely possible for a teaching-learning "happening" to appear successful in all respects (that is, the teacher may be teaching effectively and the child may be learning thoroughly) and yet have a serious flaw, namely, the failure to foster independence. Classroom teachers frequently complain (and it is a just complaint): "I know he is not dull. He can learn, but he can't do a blessed thing without my standing over him!"

It is surprising that with our ever-increasing knowledge of computerization and task analyses, very little has been said about programming for independence. And yet, upon reflection, aren't there some sequential elements which would be instrumental in enabling the child to function with greater independence? To begin with, a teacher must learn to separate a child's skill in mastering some new aspect of subject matter from his ability to work independently. In all likelihood it is too much to expect a child who is immature and overly dependent to work with some difficult material which has not previously been learned—and to do it by himself. A good sequence would be for the teacher to utilize material which the child has completely mastered for the initial independent work periods. There is a "trade-off" here. A sacrifice is made in that we deliberately encourage the child to work at—i.e., learn—that which he already knows! But we do it so that he can *learn* to function more independently. The first sequential element, then, is the "level" of the task: start with "success assured" activities and gradually increase the complexity. Another consideration is the type of pupil response inherent in the task. Activities which are repetitive and manipulative (e.g., sorting, matching, assembling, constructing) are recommended initially; these may gradually move towards more abstractness. The time dosages should be regulated so that in the beginning the independent work training sessions are relatively brief in duration. It may be necessary to sequentialize the number of distracting elements; that is, at first, sensory stimuli (auditory, visual, tactile) may have to be reduced to the bare essentials, then slowly increased as the child grows in his ability to work independently.

The degree of supervision is a tremendously important consideration in sequentializing for independence. Should the teacher offer total guidance and supervision, merely observe, or simply "step back"? An excellent example illustrating this consideration is the teaching of a child to ride a two-wheeled bicycle. The teacher-child relationship in this specific example, in a real sense, typifies the entire education process. At first, the instructor (teacher, friend, parent, etc.) places his hand on the rear of the bicycle seat, pushing, guiding, supervising, and offering total support, as he runs alongside the child. At this point the child is pedaling, but almost passively, since the instructor's "push" determines the speed. The child is learning to balance, but it doesn't matter; it is impossible to fall since the teacher is holding the bicycle and can correct any balancing errors. The second step occurs when the teacher relaxes his grip somewhat. He still holds the seat but now is "feeling" what the child does rather than controlling the entire ride. Should the child ride "incorrectly" (steer improperly, pedal too fast or too slowly, or begin to fall), the teacher can make the necessary corrections. Then the teacher, observing that the child is becoming more proficient, releases his grip almost imperceptibly so that the child is unaware that the teacher is no longer touching the bicycle; he finally runs alongside the child, observing, correcting verbally, and extending moral support, but the child is solo-ing. There are two aspects involved in this illustration:

1. the teacher, by his knowledge of the subject matter, helps the child technically; and
2. by his attitude and very presence, he helps the child psychologically. (The direction of supervision is from total to nominal and finally to none.)

Many teachers use this sequence without necessarily being aware of it. For example, a teacher instructing a child in penmanship may at first place his right hand over the child's right hand (the child is holding a pencil) and guide so thoroughly that he is actually writing for the child. Then the teacher relaxes his grip, but can (via his kinesthetic sense) tell when the child is about to make an error, and put the child "back on course". Finally, the teacher removes his hand completely from the child's, still observing, but now allowing him to write independently.

Whether or not a child has mastered a subject matter sufficiently so that he no longer needs the teacher's assistance is only one facet of the overall topic of independent functioning. Other equally important facets are value systems (How does he opt to spend his leisure time? What goals does he pursue? What causes does he embrace?); personality (What kind of decisions does he make? How creative is he? Is he outgoing or introverted?); and psychological make-up (Do emotional problems interfere with the nurturing of productive work habits? Does he assert himself? Does he show initiative? Is he *too* independent?).

A pitfall which the teacher who instructs one child at a time must avoid is the emergence of an overly dependent child, attached strongly (perhaps neurotically) to the teacher, and who believes that he can learn only if this particular instructor remains his teacher. A key factor in averting this situation is the teacher's awareness of the concept of replication. In essence, this means that whatever this teacher does for the child, other teachers should be able to do. In whatever manner the child communicates, performs, and learns with this teacher, he should be able to do likewise with other instructors. There should be no mystical bonds between teacher and child wherein only that particular teacher can understand and motivate him. Aware of this aim, the teacher can from the outset, initiate a system of responses and reactions on the part of the child which would be instantly clear to any observer. For example, suppose a handicapped child, having no speech at all and only limited use of his hands is encouraged to communicate by "writing" as the teacher holds his unsteady hand. Now this might have been a good idea in the beginning, but as it continues month in and month out, perhaps year in and year out, it might turn out that the teacher's strong emotional involvement causes him—albeit subconsciously—actually to do the writing himself and give the child credit for it! It would have been wiser for the teacher to hit upon some communication style which could be observed and understood by all and replicated by all. For example, establish a "yes-no" response, or capitalize upon the child's ability to focus his eyes upon a given object (e.g., ask him to look at the card or the object which he selects as an answer). In cases wherein the tutor is the only source of formal education for the child (e.g., homebound, "teacher–mom" programs, hospital instruction) it is usually desirable to change teachers periodically thus reducing the likelihood of the child's becoming too attached and dependent upon a particular instructor.

There is an extra "bonus" in striving to foster independence. The teacher, in attempting to set up blocks of time in which the child works by himself, must reciprocally diminish discussion time. Now it is well-known that most lessons are characterized by an abundance of verbalism: discussions, questions and answers, lectures, etc., and that this often leads to boredom and inattention. By providing for variety—namely, some independent activity—the teacher is, in effect, making the lesson more interesting.

In helping the pupil function with greater independence in the course of one teacher–one child instructional settings, the teacher is receiving excellent preparation for his future work with classrooms of children. Group instruction, by its very nature, dictates that a teacher cannot give *all* pupils his undivided attention at *all* times. The only stipulation should be that those children in the class who are not talking with the teacher—and therefore are "doing something else"—are working in a genuinely productive manner.

COMMUNICATION CONSIDERATIONS

Dewey (1969) believes that the process of transmission effects the existence of society, this transmission—that is, education—occurs via communication, and that communication is a process modifying the disposition of both participating parties, the teacher as well as the learner. Certainly, a consideration of the problems and practices involved in the communication between teacher and child is vital as one seeks to improve teaching competency.

Teachers' Verbalisms

It has been stated repeatedly that teachers, generally, are given to excessive verbalism. An analysis of "what goes on" in most classroom lessons reveals a preponderance of discussion, verbal explanations, questions and answers, etc. Now this can be detrimental to children if some modifications are not made to accommodate their "out of tune", individual language styles which may exist as a function of either cultural differences or specific language handicaps. For example, the disadvantaged child may be inexperienced in dealing with large quantities of adult speech (Riessman, 1962, 82). In addition, he has often had meager opportunities to correct his early verbalizations via the feedback of being attended to, heard, and corrected (John and Goldstein, 1967). Finally, he may have inferior habits of hearing, seeing, and thinking because his environment did not teach him to attend to the essence of what is being said and what is happening (Havighurst, 1966, 19). Siegel (1969, 7) explains that the minimally brain damaged child may have communication problems stemming from

"1. perseveration—a tendency to repeat a subject or 'talk a subject to death,'

2. impulsivity—lack of self-control when silence is appropriate,

3. 'feedback difficulty'—inability to determine readily the effect of his own conversational contributions upon others,

4. egocentricity—too much talking about 'me',

5. distractibility—talking about irrelevant subjects, and

6. minor speech problems related to articulatory defects or faulty auditory perception."

Some remedial strategies, techniques, and principles for amelioration of communication and language disorders in children have been suggested. A child in a regular classroom who has some hearing loss can be helped by: allowing him to sit where he can hear, having teachers and classmates face the light when talking, and using clear and distinct articulation (Streng, 1962, 293). Hallahan (1970, 4-9) suggests that the same remedial procedures which are believed to be helpful in coping with the language and overall cognitive deficits of the hyperkinetic minimally brain-injured child (e.g., minimizing extraneous stimuli, reducing classroom space, providing color cues to heighten attention, etc.) may be employed equally advantageously in remediating language and cognitive deficits among the disadvantaged. (The rationale is that their behavioral problems are similar: distractibility, hyperactivity, impulsivity.) Barsh (1965, 339) believes that communication strategies of the teacher can improve the child's language and listening skills: minimizing the language of directions to the level of bare essentials, at times reducing them to virtual "telegraphic speech"; avoiding ambiguous words; providing gestures to accompany words; maintaining visual contact with the child when addressing him; avoiding talking to the child when he is in the midst of some performance (some children find it extremely difficult to listen and "do" at the same time); and even touching the child as a signal for him to begin listening. Siegel (1969, 90) suggests that changes in tempo of speech—moving from slow to somewhat more rapid speech, from soft to louder, from activities requiring listening to those entailing doing—can often be helpful in preventing behavioral problems and in enhancing the interest of the lesson.

Attention is very much a function of interest; hence the teacher should endeavor to heighten the child's interest, thereby promoting attention, which, in turn, fosters productive communication. Some interest-promoting techniques, in addition to employing a change in speech tempo, are: regulating time dosages; varying the kinds of activities; providing for some physical movement of the child; using audio-visual aids and the unit method of instruction;

employing a "game" format; injecting humor in the educational experiences of the child; personalizing the lesson by becoming aware of the individual child and his background; etc.

Some overall principles emerge and these should of course be stated:

1. TALK LESS FREQUENTLY! (This is the prime rule.)
2. Make sure the child can hear and is listening.
3. Talk in small doses.
4. Talk concisely and precisely, avoiding ambiguity.
5. Talk slowly.
6. Talk softly.
7. Employ speech tempo and volume changes.
8. Heighten the child's interest.

The mere stating of these principles, however, does not really insure that the teacher will adopt them. He may very well learn them, study them, consider them—but never develop a genuine feeling for them. If this feeling is neither created nor nurtured, the teacher does not actually change in attitude, in personality and in teaching style. However, by teaching—and observing—one child at a time, the teacher will be able to witness the specific kinds (and degrees) of communication problems, their effects upon the individual child, and to devise remedial strategies, techniques, and teaching modifications. MOST IMPORTANT, SINCE THE PRINCIPLE OF FEEDBACK OPERATES MORE RELIABLY DURING THE INTERACTION OF THE TEACHER WITH A SINGLE CHILD THAN WITH GROUPS OF CHILDREN, THE TEACHER CAN ACQUIRE THE COMMUNICATION HABITS WHICH CAN FOSTER TEACHING EXCELLENCE, RENDERING HIM EFFECTIVE WITH GROUPS AS WELL AS WITH INDIVIDUAL CHILDREN, WITH THE "NORMAL" CHILD AS WELL AS THOSE WITH LANGUAGE PROBLEMS.

Handling Questions and Answers

A large part of the teaching day is devoted to the process of questioning and answering. The queries and responses are usually verbal, and the general order is for the teacher to pose the question to the child, who then attempts to provide an answer. The most obvious function of such questions and answers is that they serve as diagnostic and evaluative instruments: What does the child know *before* instruction? What does he know *after* the lesson? This process of questioning and answering is vital to the child's classroom education since it requires a total mutual involvement between teacher and child. Moreover, in answering, the child delivers an "observable behavior," one which the teacher can readily use as feedback data as he attempts to refine his instructional skills. The non-verbal communication of the child—that is, the *manner* in which he responds as opposed to the sheer content—provides additional cues to the teacher about the child (anxieties, fears, self-concept, degree of confidence, coping mechanisms, stress thresholds and reactions, etc.).

Some of the criteria for effective questions and questioning set forth by Treatman (1957, 157) are: the questions should be concise, clear and thought-provoking; they should be presented in logical order; they should not be too many nor too few and they should be distributed among the children; sufficient time and attention should be given to the answer and care should be exercised by the teacher in handling the answers.

There are specific suggestions concerned with the process of questioning and answering, which, if explored and entertained fully, might result in the teacher's "tightening" and refining of his methodology. Attitudes and techniques can emerge which will improve the teacher's ability to frame productive questions, and, at the same time, get maximum "mileage" from the child's answers.

Guessing. Many children learn to *guess* rather than *answer*. It is easy to see why. If they guess, they at least have the chance to be correct, whereas, if they say "I don't know," their "failure" is both obvious and total. The child who has been conditioned to guess instead of think each time a question is asked, must be re-trained. One approach is to ask failure-free questions such as: "What is your favorite T.V. program?" "How did you spend your vacation?" "What game will you play during recess?" "How do you think Columbus felt when he sighted land?" etc. There are no incorrect answers to these questions. It is of utmost importance that the teacher avoid having any preconceived "right" answer in mind, lest he convey either verbally or through body language, that he is not satisfied with the child's response. By providing the child with lots of experience in handling these questions the teacher is teaching him that all questions are not "out to get him" and the pupil is learning that it is neither dangerous nor threatening to *think,* and to express his thoughts in his answer.

Children often indulge in guessing during written work as well as in oral question and answer periods. Generally, written work is not corrected immediately. This lack of corrective feedback can reinforce the attitude that "anything goes" and that one answer is as good as another. A simple remediation technique which tends to make the child more responsible for his decisions is to require him to verify his answer by referring to an exact portion of the text. This is done by instructing the child, after he has indicated the written answer, to go back to the text and place the number of the question in the margin next to the text's line which verifies the answer.

There are exceptions to the "no guessing" rule. Gisonti (1971, 73, 74) points out that children from low socioeconomic areas are often so reluctant to take the chance of mispronouncing a word during reading that they hesitate too long. He advises teachers to reinforce the *efforts* of the child to communicate, thus encouraging a spontaneity in answering and bolstering feelings of self-confidence through the successful experience of simply *trying*. Initially, then,

—◇ 1 ◇—

Each year the little girls of Japan have a holiday which makes 2
them very happy. It is called the Feast of Dolls, and is held dur- 1
3 ing the early part of March. The feast lasts three days and during 6
that time the little girls are allowed to play with all their dolls. 4
These dolls are not only their own but those that belonged to their mothers, their grandmothers, and also their great-grandmothers. Most Japanese girls have many dolls and are very care- 5
7 ful of them. During the feast, the dolls are dressed in their best clothes and placed on stands so that people may admire them. When the three days are over, the old dolls are put carefully 8
away until the next year.

1. This holiday is called the Feast of (a) Kites (b) Flags (c) Dolls (d) Fishes
2. The holiday is celebrated in (a) China (b) Japan (c) the United States (d) Germany
3. The feast is held in (a) May (b) December (c) June (d) March
4. At this time the girls play with their (a) dolls (b) brothers (c) pets (d) toys
5. How many dolls do the little girls have? (a) a few (b) none (c) one (d) many
6. How many days does the feast last? (a) one (b) two (c) three (d) four
7. Little Japanese girls handle their dolls (a) carefully (b) carelessly (c) roughly (d) playfully
8. At the end of the feast the old dolls are (a) given away (b) kept on stands (c) put away (d) played with

these children should be encouraged to guess. For many minimally brain-injured children, on the other hand, the guessing style should be discouraged in deference to their need for structure and predictability in the learning situation. There is a temporal dimension here. The child who may need encouragement to guess in the beginning, should, at some later date, be led towards more critical thinking.

Again, the choice between encouraging guessing (thus emphasizing rapidity of response) and stressing the contemplating style of answering will depend upon the teacher's ability to observe the child and sense his style and his needs.

Pausing. A child frequently pauses before answering. The teacher surmises that the delay is not attributable to the child's collecting his thoughts." Instead, it seems that he is merely uncertain and is selecting, entirely by whim, one of many alternatives—each of which he is equally doubtful—rather than the correct answer. Clearly, the teacher should intervene. It is imperative that the child's slow and unsure answering style change to one of assurance and precision. An excellent technique is to use questions which are success-assured, not in the sense that there are no possible wrong answers to them, but that the teacher is certain that the child is very apt to know the answers (e.g., "What is the color of this apple?" "What shape is a baseball?" "Which feels softer—this cotton or this piece of metal?" etc.). These kinds of questions require very little contemplation and it is quite possible that they will evoke answers which not only are correct, but are stated quickly and with confidence. A helpful suggestion is to intermingle these questions with those which have in the past been met with delay and uncertainty in responding on the part of the child (e.g., arithmetic drill questions). In other words, the "easy" questions, those which demonstrate to the child that there is an exactness to answers, are juxtaposed with the more difficult ones. The child is experiencing success in dealing with them and therefore is rapidly moving towards an appreciation of precision (i.e., an answer is either right or wrong and there is often only one correct answer to a given question), and reciprocally away from guessing. Because of this juxtaposition, the probability that the child will improve his response style is greatly enhanced.

The teacher must learn to recognize strategies employed by the child, either consciously or subconciously, which tend to mask the slowness and uncertainty of response. A favorite one is the child's repeating of part of the question in order to get more time to think of the answer: the teacher asks, "How much is nine and six?" The child begins to answer (slowly), "Nine and . . . (pause) six are . . . (pause). . . . ." Obviously, it is not necessary for the child to repeat, "nine and six are . . ."; the goal is for the answer to be given correctly and *quickly**. The teacher should tactfully lead the child into seeing that answering "nine and six are. ." is tantamount to stalling and that it would be better to increase and/or vary drill procedures in such a way as to reduce the time interval between question and answer.

Response time. The time interval between question and answer can be a revealing clue to the teacher, but it is necessary to interpret this interval correctly. Does a hesitating response indicate that the child is having difficulty with the question or does it reflect a thoughtful, "slow and steady" style? The teacher can solve this

* Note: Of course, there are times when children should be led to contemplation, consideration, and analysis before blurting out the first thing that comes to mind. The adage "think before you speak" is well taken in many situations. This does not negate the fact that there are other instances (e.g., arithmetic drill questions, spelling words, factual geography questions,) which should not require deep reasoning, but merely memory and retrieval. At these times, only prompt responses are appropriate. During his pausing strategy, the child may very well be figuring out—by counting on his fingers, picturing objects, or by some other means—the sum of nine and six, and *he may be figuring accurately.* The point, however, is that he still doesn't *know* the answer. Ultimately, "knowing" the answer to "$9 + 6 = \square$" involves pure memory.

puzzle by establishing a basal for response time and style in this manner:

1. ascertain that the pupil thoroughly knows the answer to a given question;
2. pose this question to the child, the answer to which demonstrates his mastery;
3. observe his manner of delivery, and note the time interlude between query and response; this is the basal.

The teacher has thus learned how the child performs when he genuinely knows the answer. Thereafter, when the child answers a question similar to the basal in complexity, level, language, emotional valence, etc., slower and more haltingly, it must be a function of his uncertainty. The teacher can then undertake necessary corrective measures.

Children vary in their ability to handle time intervals between questions and answers, depending upon their emotional makeup. Some emotionally disturbed children spend the time interval feeling insecure, "on-the-spot," hostile, negative, extremely self-conscious. Every moment that transpires heightens their self-consciousness and embarrassment, and they are rendered unable to use this time to think productively and calmly. It would be wise for the teacher to recognize this problem, and to eliminate pause periods for these children. This can be done by immediately providing further verbal hints, telling the child the answer at once, or changing the subject. The teacher must do this quickly, avoiding the painful pause at all costs.

There are other children (for example, those with slight articulatory defects or with mild aphasia) presenting occasional difficulty in recalling a word—"I have it on the tip of my tongue"—who *need* the pause, are not self-conscious about their slower style, and who handle the pause period productively. The teacher should, of course, exercise patience in these cases, communicating to the child—perhaps in words, but especially in manner—that the delay is perfectly acceptable. "Take it easy," "We have lots of time," "You're important and we'll wait for you," are all feelings that should be conveyed to the child.

Another important consideration is the length of the spoken answer. The teacher ought to encourage the overly talkative child to speak to the point, concisely, and in small doses; words must not become a substitute for doing or, even worse, for thinking. On the other hand, the shy, withdrawn child should be urged to qualify, embellish, lengthen, and "explain" his answer as he is led away from monosyllabic, barely audible intonations towards a more effective speech style. Again, knowing the child will enable the teacher to determine how to help him and in which direction to lead him.

Unwitting clues. The teacher should avoid providing unwitting clues to the child—facial expressions; tone of voice; unconscious lip movements, mouthing part of or the entire answer; nodding his head; actually looking at the correct answer (e.g., a specific word on the blackboard); etc. Often pupils learn to "read" teachers' clues and thereby answer correctly, but without understanding what is being taught.

Degrees of knowing. There are varying degrees of understanding. A pupil may just barely understand, holding on to "just a little piece" of the material being taught; he may understand fairly well but not thoroughly, missing many of the subtleties, ramifications, and conceptualized principles; or grasp completely, achieving a high degree of mastery. The teacher, then, must realize the possibilty of the child's knowing and yet not *really* knowing; there are techniques which can take into account these varying degrees of mastery:

A child who is only partially sure may still produce the right answer. The teacher rewards him immediately. The child is satisfied. The teacher, believing that the child has learned, is obviously pleased. And most unfortunately, the question-answer period for that item is over. The teacher should train himself *not* to reward—or give any other clue—immediately after the child's response, but to wait a few moments. A child who answers the question, "How much is seven times six?" with "forty-two," may follow his initial unsure response with "forty-three," "forty-four," and other such guesses provided the teacher does not react at once to his first try. It is as though the teacher, by refraining from comment, is asking the child to "stick by his guns." If the child *really* knows the answer, the pause does not throw him off. If the teacher hadn't paused, however, he might never know of the child's tenuous grasp and would therefore have no reason to initiate remediation.

The kinds of questions a teacher asks can often help to reveal the degree of mastery. A child who may handle a "yes-no" question correctly may fail in more thought-provoking ones. A multiple-choice test item generally requires less mastery than does an open-ended question. By and large, essays warrant more thought than do objective type test items. Asking a child to explain *how* he arrived at an arithmetic example's answer may unearth problems that may not otherwise be evident. It is interesting and helpful to note that in a nurse's tutoring study in which student nurses from disadvantaged areas were tutored in biological sciences by proficient college students, the single most effective instructional method in the opinions of the tutees and the project evaluators was the tutor's request to "explain it back to me" (Glanzrock, 1969).

Certainly, memory is one way of determining degree of grasp. When a child forgets some previously "learned" material quickly, it is highly likely that he never *mastered* it initially.

Reading too much into child's answer. At times, a teacher sets up a teaching-learning situation, the child is led towards performing a particular "observable objective," but the teacher misinterprets the significance and meaning of the child's response. It is not unlike the story told of the reseacher who, having trained a flea to hop upon verbal command, proceeds to sever pairs of the flea's legs. At each point he commands "Hop." The last pair of legs finally severed, the flea does not obey the order "Hop," whereupon the researcher concludes, "This experiment proves dramatically that when a flea's legs are cut off he becomes deaf!"

Suppose a teacher is instructing a child to recognize one object and two objects. The teacher constructs sets of domino cards, say, ten, for each number. He prepares ten cards with one dot ⚀ and ten cards with two dots ⚁ . After some instruction, the child is able to respond with 100% accuracy, answering either "one" or "two" when shown a card. Now the teacher may conclude from this that the child fully understands "two-ness" and can recognize two objects as distinct from any other number of them. This may, of course, very well be the case. However, it is also possible that the child understands the concept of "one" only, and that his selection of the "two" card was made on the basis of *differentness:* "It is different from *one,* and since the only possibilities dealt with here are *one* and *two,* it must be *two.*" To discover the true degree of mastery, the teacher can introduce some three-dot cards ⚂ . The child may then show considerable confusion between *"two"* and *"three."* The point is that he never fully understood *"two,"* but this became apparent to the teacher only after *"three"* was introduced.

Using humor in multiple-choice alternatives. The incorrect alternates in multiple-choice items are often incorrect because of absurdities or incongruities. There is an element of humor in the absurd, and this can be capitalized upon. A shy child, one who is not talkative or outgoing, who does not usually volunteer information, frequently "loosens up" when asked why he rejected an absurd alternative. Consider the following:

I LOOKED IN THE SKY AND SAW A ____________.
a) wind b) cloud c) submarine d) air

The child correctly underlines "cloud." If asked why he didn't select "submarine," he may suddenly smile, relax, and say "submarines can't fly."

The inherent humor of absurdities can also be used with capable older children. This can be done by encouraging them to compose their own multiple-choice test items, thus fostering creative writing while providing educational experience in the given subject area.

PSYCHOLOGICAL CONSIDERATIONS

Psychological Pitfalls of Tutoring

It is well-known that the one-to-one instructional setting offers considerable emotional security to the pupil. There are many reasons for this: The child who is self-conscious in the midst of a classroom of children may very likely relax in the presence of just one person, the teacher; the child who is starved for affection may, at some given point, be unprepared to share the teacher's attention with others; the child who is easily distractible may well find the classroom (and its attendant sensory stimuli bombardment) overwhelming and thus anxiety-provoking, whereas the one teacher-one child ratio can prove more relaxing. Despite all of these emotional positives featured in the tutoring process, there is another side of the coin—some very definite pitfalls exist:

1. For some emotionally handicapped children, the classroom setting may offer some degree of security in that they can mingle with other children, withdraw at times from the group, step back into the center of activities when they feel entirely ready to do so, and, in general, are not under the close, constant scrutiny of the teacher. In the tutoring sessions, however, the child is, in a sense,

always "under the gun," being the sole focal point of the teacher's unrelenting attention and gaze. The sheer proximity of tutor to tutee can for some children be frightening. Capping all of these factors is the likelihood that the adult tutor (teacher, teacher-trainee, paraprofesssional, parent) is often viewed as an authority figure in a negative sense: The child in all probability has met considerable failure in school. (If not, then why has he been referred for tutoring?) He becomes negatively attuned to school, school procedures, and school authority figures.

2. Inherent in one-to-one teaching is that the nature of the setting emphasizes the "differentness" of the child. Most children do not require tutoring, but he does. Ironically, then, providing the child with the very service he needs can be ego-deflating in that it sets him apart—at least in his mind—from his peers.

3. The teacher who is instructing a single child, and feeling duty-bound to "produce," may push the child beyond his capabilities. The entire concept of educational and psychological readiness is a vital one here and must be thoroughly understood by the teacher. Some of the consequences of pushing a child who isn't equipped to go ahead may be frustration, poor teacher-child or parent-child relationship, poor attitude toward school, development of emotional or learning blocks, or at the very least, a waste of time.

4. The one-to-one teaching format is, literally, a very close relationship. There is the danger, therefore, of the teacher and child becoming too attached to one another with the resultant decrease in objectivity. (See pages 129-130).

5. Regarding the overall consideration of employing a good mental hygiene approach, the one teacher–one child instructional setting is an ideal one, in general. That is, the teacher is in an advantageous position to observe the emotional "highs" and "lows" of the child and to make the necessary adjustments. He can foster

feelings of self-esteem by personalizing the lesson, gearing the syllabus to the child's interests and needs, and by judicious use of praise. He can reduce anxiety (and this too is necessary for the emergence of a positive self-concept) by regulating time dosages, providing for some "success-assured" activities, and injecting humor into the lesson. However, there is one specific area in which the tutoring setting can prove harmful to the child's ego. At times, the supervisor of the teacher, teacher-trainee, or tutor observes the lesson. During this observation the tutor may feel compelled to "explain things" about the child or his progress to the supervisor (instead of simply going ahead with the lesson). It happens that remarks are made—with no malice intended—but which can nevertheless have adverse effects upon the child's emotional well-being. The child can be hurt in two ways: (1) talking about his problems in front of him *as though he were not present* is a form of dehumanization, and (2) the content of the statements may be insulting and/or embarrassing. The following are verbatim examples of comments made by teachers and trainees to their supervisors in the presence of the sole child:

"This child is not mentally retarded, he's just emotionally retarded."

"Please try to get a man teacher for this child. His father died recently."

"Because he's poor in English, I've discontinued teaching him French."

"He *finally* got that."

"He can't work at the table. Notice?" (This was said about a child in a full leg cast. The handicapping condition did not have to be pointed out since it was obvious.)

"I am trying to help Tony lose his Puerto Rican accent."

"He's learning to read." (This remark was made about an educable mentally retarded child with a severe reading disorder who was 15 years old. The teacher, of course, desired to explain that some progress had recently been made, but isn't it obviously ego-deflating to a child of that age to be told that he is merely *learning* to read?)

"I write—his mother translates." (This was said concerning the same 15 year old boy. The teacher wanted to show that she had developed this technique of helping him, but again, isn't it embarrassing to the child for others to discover in *front of him* that he cannot read the teacher's writing and that his mother must translate it for him?)

"This youngster isn't dull. He can learn. But he's inclined to be lazy." (This remark might well be insulting for any child. In this case it was especially distasteful since the child involved was a Black teenager who was undoubtedly all too familiar with the stereotype racial slur—unwitting on the part of the teacher but just as painful and maligning as if it had been pronounced by some bigot.)

Avoiding the Pitfalls

It should be pointed out that although these pitfalls are indeed possible, they are by no means absolutely predestined. Their prevention rests largely upon the degree of sensitivity for the child engendered in the teacher.

The teacher (or tutor) can takes steps towards minimizing the child's feelings of being "under the gun." Some means of achieving this would be: (1) to step back occasionally, thus letting the child do some independent work, (2) to walk around at times, thus literally "getting away" from the child, (3) to provide for the child's physical movement, allowing him to leave the work arena to erase the board, get some material, walk over to the window to make some observations, etc. (4) to begin with short tutoring sessions, gradually increasing the length. The problem of the child's viewing the instructor as an overpowering authority figure can be mitigated by the teacher's artistry in blending permissiveness with structure. The child needs both. The teacher must deliberately create situations in which the child can "win a few": A question such as "Would you prefer using the text or the workbook now?" gives the child a choice and yet guarantees that whatever decision he makes, it will be compatible with the teacher's goals. This would not have been the case had the teacher posed the open-end question: "What would you like to do now?" In the same vein, the teacher, upon surmising that the child is going through an "I won't complete all the work" phase, can purposely overassign (e.g, ask the child to perform three arithmetic examples, when in reality the teacher's plans require the completion of only two of them.) The point here is that if the child can "save face," the teacher will seem less threatening.

Feelings of self-consciousness, "differentness," and self-deprecation which the child may associate with the fact that he requires tutoring will very likely diminish if the teacher, tutor, or parent handle the situation in a matter-of-fact manner. Point out that other children, too, at times, may require additional instruction. Make the child aware of his strengths instead of emphasizing deficits. Help him realize that this assistance is temporary rather than ongoing. Present the tutoring service as a privilege (perhaps capitalizing on the fact that many of the elite are educated in this manner). Finally, endeavor to make the one teacher–one child instructional sessions as pleasurable as possible so that the child might actually look forward to them.

The effective teacher does not pressure a child to perform beyond his readiness level. What is needed is a clear understanding of "where the child is at" at the moment (i.e., an educational profile showing strengths, weaknesses, and levels of performance). The teacher must be entirely conversant with readiness programs from a subject matter viewpoint (e.g., reading readiness, non-numerical arithmetic concepts, penmanship readiness). He must be equally aware of the concept of readiness in terms of helping the child "learn to learn" (e.g., attention span, following directions, etc.). The problem of how to help the child who doesn't seem ready is intimately linked with the teacher's thorough understanding of the subject area and an appreciation of the task requirements. For example: A child doesn't seem to be ready for phonic blending. He can read and pronounce "p" and "ay" but simply cannot put them together. The teacher points to the "p" and the child gives the correct sound; he points to the "ay," and the child again gives the correct sound. The teacher points faster and faster in the hope that the blend will "take". The child reads faster and faster: "p ——— ay," "p —— ay," "p — ay," p – ay," but he still can't recognize the word! If the teacher thoroughly understood phonics and Speech, he would not use the plosive letter *p* initially. He would instead start with a consonant which can be held a long time (e. g., f,l,m,n,r,s,v). The child is shown the *m*. He then has a much better chance of recognizing (i.e., hearing *may* than *pay*. And so the question of "Is the child ready?" is often synonymous with "Does the teacher know where to begin?"

The pitfall of speaking in a derogatory manner about the child in his presence can be avoided if the teacher would take the following two precautions: First, remember that when the supervisor comes to observe the lesson, she basically desires to witness the teaching-learning process, not to hear explanations about the child. The teacher, after attending to the social amenities of the greetings and/or introduction of supervisor to tutee, should simply proceed with the lesson as though it were unobserved. A good idea is for the teacher to carry with him, in addition to the written lesson plans, some case history data concerning the child and to present these to the supervisor, thus eliminating the need for discussing the child in his presence. Secondly, should the teacher still feel that some comments concerning the child must be made during the lesson, the words should be chosen with great care. "He's *improving* in reading," is better than "He's *learning* to read." "He likes classwork better than homework," is less incriminating than "He never does any homework." "He has a habit of considering a question very carefully before answering," is not in the least derogatory, whereas "He's very slow in answering," may easily be interpreted by the child as an insult.

Motivation and Attention

The dual factors of attention and motivation are basic—and very likely, the *only* ingredients required—to insure optimal learning. In other words, given a child with a specific set of strengths and weaknesses as a learner, and a teacher with his own set of pedagogical strengths and weaknesses, then if "only the child would pay attention," and if "only he wanted to learn," optimal education (within the framework of the given circumstances) would indeed occur. The one-to-one instructional setting is the ideal initial one for the teacher to develop skill in motivating children and in capturing their attention. Just as the teacher, by working with only one child, can often determine *how* he is failing and *why* he is failing, the teacher can also observe equally fully the factors of non-motivation and inattention. Given a distractible tutee, the teacher can actually follow his gaze, observe the objects with which he is fidgeting, or determine the sounds which are distracting him—thereby detecting the exact source of his inattention. The teacher literally "sees" the child's inattention and can then begin to supply appropriate ameliorative measures. Similarly, the teacher of a single child has the opportunity to pursue his non-motivation to its source and is thus in an advantageous position to effect attitudinal changes. Moreover, since it is very probably true that the mechanism of feedback is much more reliable in teaching one child than when instructing groups of children, the teacher—by hypothesizing and trying out remedial measures, evaluating their effect upon the child, and making a series of refinements based upon successive observations—can finally zoom in on the most effective means of dealing with the child's inattention and poor motivation. The knowledge thus gained initially while teaching one child at a time will stand the teacher in good stead later as he endeavors to motivate and to interest a classroom of children.

Contraindications

Because there are some pitfalls inherent in the one teacher-one child setting, in view of the fact that some parents may tutor their children unsupervised and when the child is young and in many ways fragile, and since individual instruction is often an optional service, it is important that any possible contraindications be enumerated:

1. Many of the contraindications are pegged to the practice of tutoring very young children in reading. Although visual problems can be aggravated by reading at any age, one should be especially cautious in initiating formal reading training with the young. Some symptoms of undected visual problems might be tilting of the head while reading, holding the printed page either too far from or too close to the eyes, covering or shutting one eye while reading, or squinting. Complaints of various kinds—e.g., words that seem to "jump," blurred or double vision, eye pain—should be checked out medically. Sties, dizziness, headaches, frequent rubbing of the eyes, and eye redness might be the signs of visual defect.

Frostig (1964, 13) found that 20% to 25% of children beginning first grade had not developed the necessary visual perception required for initial reading, arithmetic, and writing programs. Bloomfield and Barnhart (1962, 3) point out that a child can indicate he has developed the muscular (ocular) skills necessary to see the small difference between letters when he can button his clothing and can see and pick up a small object (say, a pin) from the floor. Clearly, it is ill-advised to push the child beyond his perceptual readiness level lest physical problems (such as headaches and eye strain) and emotional problems ensue.

2. In most cases it is a good idea to postpone the tutoring program if the child seems to resist it. He may simply state that he doesn't want it, or he may show his feelings in other ways (nervousness, hostility, negativism, excessive dawdling when getting ready for the lesson, etc.). Although it is true that part of maturing is learning that, at times, one must do things which are not necessarily enjoyable, it is wise to at least consider the child's feelings. Sometimes, instead of totally discontinuing the program, an adjustment in logistics is needed: e.g., a change in the tutoring day, a change to an earlier or later hour, arranging for the tutor to conduct the lesson in the child's home (thus eliminating the child's travel time), etc.

3. If the child is beginning to be (or feel) over-serviced, it may be desirable to postpone the tutoring program. Many of the learning disabled, particularly, those in the middle class socioeconomic bracket, in addition to their daily school attendance, may receive speech therapy, psychotherapy, and possibly "patterning" (a structured, ongoing, rather time-consuming regimen somewhat akin to physiotherapy). Other commitments might be dance lessons, religious instruction, Saturday play groups, and Scout groups. If the child views tutoring as an added pressure, little educational gains are likely, while conversely, emotional problems are apt to result.

4. Tutoring should be discontinued if it keeps the child from having a *total* program. He needs social and recreational experiences as well as educational ones, informal as well as formal ones, and above all, he needs some privacy and "free time."

5. If a mother who embarks upon a program of tutoring her child feels emotionally unprepared to do so (some signs being anger and impatience), she should end these sessions. It turns out that some parents who are too emotionally involved to effectively tutor their own children are more successful when teaching other children. Hence "trading" children for tutoring sessions might prove to be a worthwhile practice.

6. Occasionally situational problems arise which suggest simply that a given session—rather than the entire individual instructional program—be cancelled. To put it differently, a child is entitled to have a "bad day" now and then, and at such times it is no great loss to merely "recess" the tutoring session.

7. A child may tire easily due to physical and/or psychological factors. He performs well before fatigue sets in. An obvious modification here would be to shorten the lesson so that it ends before the onset of fatigue, boredom, and frustration.

It is recommended that those individuals making the decision for either initiating or discontinuing a child's tutoring program (i.e., school administrators, parents, etc.) seek the counseling, when necessary, of the appropriate professionals. These would include general practictioners, psychiatrists or psychologists, eye specialists, speech therapists, etc. The point is that deciding against tutoring is just as much of a decision as opting for it. Hence, when in doubt, professional guidance should be sought.

Education and Behavior

There is a large overlap between "learning" and "behavior." One term can be subsumed under the other—i.e., learning is a form of behavior, while behavior is a resultant of learning.

It is helpful to look at this relationship from the standpoint of nurturing the child educationally and psychologically: if one helps a child to learn, then his behavior will probably improve proportionately since anxiety has been reduced and self-concept strengthened.. Conversely, if anxiety-reduction and inceased self-esteem could occur through some other means, the child would probably become a better learner since there would be less psychological interference and greater motivation.

From the standpoint of the teacher, there is a similar relationship. That is to say, *teaching* and *managing* greatly coincide. Very often, a teacher who is poor at managing (i.e., controlling) a classroom of children, improves in "discipline," not by attacking the problem of negative behavior directly, but by growing more skilled in pedagogical techniques. He becomes so sure of his subject matter and so skilled in methodology (particularly in developing a sequence of steps based upon the task requirements) that he virtually exudes, "Come on, now. We just don't have time for that kind of behavior. I know exactly what you need and how to teach it to you." The teacher's own self-confidence, purposeful behavior, and organization bring about, in turn, more mature conduct on the part of the class. Again, if it happened that the pupils were well-behaved for reasons unrelated to the teacher's instructional expertise (say, a function of his organizational and management skills), he would probably grow in teaching ability since by not having to contend with discipline problems, he could now devote all of his efforts and energies towards improving his teaching proficiency.

The one teacher-one child instructional mode is an ideal proving—and *improving*—ground from all viewpoints. Some children may require individual instruction before becoming effective classroom learners. *All* teachers will be better prepared to instruct groups of children and to deal with their behavioral and psychological problems if they first become experienced in teaching one child at a time.

References

Ausubel, David P., "A Teaching Strategy for Culturally Deprived Pupils: Cognitive and Motivational Considerations," in Joe L. Frost and Glenn R. Hawkes (eds.), *The Disadvantaged Child,* Boston: Houghton Mifflin Co., 1966, pp. 237-244.

Barry, Hortense, *Teaching the Young Aphasic Child,* Washington: Alexander Graham Bell Association for the Deaf, Inc., 1961.

Barsch, Ray H., "Six Factors in Learning," in Jerome Hellmuth (ed.), *Learning Disorders,* Volume I, Seattle, Washington: Special Child Publications, Inc. 1965, pp. 329-343.

Blackman, Leonard, "Research Need in the Special Education of the Mentally Retarded," *Exceptional Children,* April, 1963, 29, 8, pp. 377-384.

Blackman, Leonard, "The Brave New World of Special Education," New York: Teachers College, Columbia University (n.d.) pp. 1-16.

Bloomfield, Leonard and Barnhart, Clarence L., *Let's Read: A Linguistic Approach,* Detroit: Wayne State University Press, 1961.

Dewey, John, "Education as a Necessity of Life," in Van Cleve Morris (ed.), *Modern Movements in Educational Philosophy,* Boston: Houghton Mifflin, 1969, pp. 134-142.

Frostig, Marianne and Horne, David, *The Frostig Program for the Development of Visual Perceptions: Teacher's Guide,* Chicago: Follett, 1964.

Gagné, Robert, M., *The Conditions of Learning,* Second Edition. New York: Holt, Rinehart and Winston, 1970.

Gattegno, Caleb, and Hinman, Dorothea, "Words in Color," in John Money (ed.), *The Disabled Reader: Education of the Dyslexic Child,* Baltimore: John Hopkins Press, 1966.

Gisonti, Frank, *Tactual-Visual Intersensory Integration and Reading Performance of Minimally Brain-Injured and Normal*

Children, unpublished Ed.D Dissertation, New York: Teachers College, Columbia University, 1971.

Glanzrock, Naomi (program director), *Nurse Tutoring Study of the City University of New York: Interim Progress Report,* Grant # NPG-326-01, June 30, 1969.

Gordon, Edmund W., quoted in *The Six-Hour Retarded Child,* A report on a conference on problems of education of children in the inner city, Aug. 10-12, 1969, The President's Committee on Mental Retardation, Office of Education, U.S. Department of Health, Education and Welfare, p. 12.

Hallahan, David P., "Cognitive Styles: Preschool Implications for the Disadvantaged," *Journal of Learning Disabilities,* Vol. 3, No. 1, Jan. 1970, pp. 4-9.

Havighurst, Robert J., "Who Are the Socially Disadvantaged?" in Joe L. Frost and Glenn R. Hawkes (eds.), *The Disadvantaged Child,* Boston: Houghton Mifflin, 1966, pp. 15-23.

John, Vera P. and Goldstein, Leo S., "The Social Context of Language Acquisition," in Jerome Hellmuth (ed.), *Disadvantaged Child,* Vol. 1, Seattle, Washington: Special Child Publications, Seattle Seguin Schools, 1967, pp. 455-469.

Lourie, Reginald S., "Experience with Therapy of Psychosomatic Problems in Infants," in Paul H. Hoch and Joseph Zubin (eds.), *Psychopathology of Childhood,* New York: Grune and Stratton, 1955.

Meacham, Merle and Wiesen, Allen, *Changing Classroom Behavior,* Scranton, Pa.: International Textbook Co., 1970.

Meidinger, Thomas, "What to Do About It," *Journal of Learning Disabilities:* Letters to the Editor, July, 1970, Vol 3, No. 7, p. 371.

Rawson, Margaret B., "Let's Get Down to the Essentials of Teaching," *Journal of Learning Disabilities, Viewpoints,* April, 1971, Vol. 4, Number 4, 224-225.

Rogers, Melvin —L., "Educational Illusions?" *New York Post:* Letters to the Editor, August 12, 1970, p. 48.

Riessman, Frank, *The Culturally Deprived Child,* New York: Harper & Row, 1962.

Siegel, Ernest, *Special Education in the Regular Classroom,* New York: John Day, 1969.

Spalding, R. B. and Spalding, W. T., *The Writing Road to Reading,* New York: Morrow, 1957.

Stern, Catherine and Gould, Toni, *Children Discover Reading,* New York: Random House, 1965.

Streng, Alice, "The Child Who Is Hard of Hearing," in James F. Magary and John R. Eichorn (eds.), *The Exceptional Child: A Book of Readings,* New York: Holt, Rinehart, and Winston, 1962.

Treatman, Paul, *Teacher's License Training Text: Assistant-to-Principal, Junior Principal, and Principal,* New York: Arco, 1957.

Van Witsen, Betty, *Perceptual Training Activities Handbook,* New York: Teachers College Press, Teachers College, Columbia University, 1967.

Chapter IV

Teaching One Child: A Strategy For Developing Teaching Excellence

THE ROLE OF THE SCHOOL ADMINISTRATOR

If one starts with the premise that *all* children require one-to-one instruction, then school administrators are doomed to frustration, since there simply isn't enough time in the day for each child in the classroom to be instructed individually. Sure, the teacher could make a valiant attempt to tutor each of his thirty to thirty-five pupils daily, but it certainly could not be an ongoing or systematic process. Fortunately, however, not all students require this approach. Consequently a virtual impossibility is transformed into a solvable—albeit, at times, difficult—problem of logistics: How can we provide tutoring for those children who need it? Should the classroom teacher do the tutoring? Or should additional personnel serve as tutors? What can be done to insure that the rest of the class does not "lose out" because of the extra attention given those pupils requiring it?

In the same way, if the school administrator attempted to plan for *all* teachers to give individual instruction, frustration would again result since the logistics would again present an insurmountable barrier. Although it is advocated that every teacher receive ongoing, guided training while teaching one child at a time, the ideal arrangement is for this to be done while the teacher is enrolled at a teacher-training institution. The administrator must concentrate upon the teacher who is inexperienced and/or inadequate. These are the ones for whom he will endeavor to provide the opportunity for tutoring as part of the in-service training process either during the school day or in in-service courses conducted after school hours.

To sum up, then, since so many advantages accrue to both tutor and tutee as a result of the one-to-one teaching setting, the school administrator must plan to accommodate those pupils who need to receive it and those teachers who need to perform it.

Providing Tutoring Experiences in the Classroom

There should be some criteria for selection. Children in regular classes who might require some individual teaching could include the underachiever, the unmotivated, the slow learner, the learning disabled, etc. A child with special health problems (e.g., poor vision or hearing, poor coordination) might benefit from tutoring. Psychological problems such as anxiety and poor self-concept are often ameliorated by the extra attention and support inherent in one-to-one teaching. Study skills and work habits (e.g., attention, initiative, orderliness, neatness, etc.) can often be strengthened by tutoring.

The referral source will usually be the classroom teacher. Tutoring can, however, be suggested by other school personnel such as the guidance counselor, the school nurse or doctor, etc. In some instances, the parents, once they are aware of the availability of additional, individual help for their child, may make the request.

The pupil selection process deserves the most careful consideration for several reasons. First, one-to-one instruction should be reserved for only those pupils who need it (after all, it is expensive and difficult to arrange; besides, many children are able to learn quite a bit by themselves and in regular group instruction, and simply do not need the "something extra" involved in the tutoring setting). Equally important, by selecting only those children who require it, we insure that the experience derived by the teacher-tutor will be of maximum benefit to him. The principle here is that one can learn more about the teaching-learning process by interning with problem learners than with "normal" pupils who require no special help.

If the tutoring is to be done in the classroom, the tutor will be the teacher, an aide (paraprofessional), a student teacher, a classmate, an older pupil in the school or even a volunteer. The school administrator can increase the likelihood that the classroom teacher will have the necessary time to offer individual instruction to one or more given pupils during class time by reducing class size, providing additional services, requesting materials which have a high "independent work" index (e.g., programmed instructional material, classroom libraries, math "labs"), making available multimedia (e.g., Educational TV, special radio programs), employing a "floating teacher" among several classes (as is done in some special education units) and, in some cases, scheduling some "free" periods (similar to preparation periods) for the teacher.

(It goes without saying that all this is expensive. The most capable administrator—talented, conscientious, energetic—will yet fail to bring about needed changes if the public does not support his efforts with appropriate funding and necessary legislation.)

Additional personnel can often be utilized to allow the child to receive tutoring and/or to allow the teacher the time to engage in tutoring. These include itinerant teachers, crisis teachers, resource room teachers, volunteers, paraprofessionals, student-teachers, teacher aides, etc. Some of this personnel will teach the rest of the class while the teacher instructs one child. Others (e.g., the resource room teacher) will provide the actual tutoring. But even here, owing to the "relief" nature of having one or several pupils removed from the classroom, the teacher himself will, to an extent, be freed to provide some tutoring to individual pupils in his classroom.

It is imperative that the administrator work to establish positive communication and attitudes between the classroom teacher and the added personnel. A student-teacher introduced into a classroom can produce either beneficial or deleterious results. A volunteer can either provide useful services or get in the way. A paraprofessional can work either with or against the classroom teacher. The resource teacher and classroom teacher can either work harmoniously or be at odds with each other.

In an Education course I taught at the University of New Mexico during the summer session of 1971, in which were enrolled school administrators, regular classroom teachers, and resource room teachers, the following term-paper question was asked:

> You are a resource teacher. A pupil in a regular class has a "problem" and is referred to the resource room. You will evaluate, diagnose and prescribe; the child will then be sent back to his regular class.
>
> a. List the kinds of problems which should be referred to the resource room.
>
> b. Choose one of these problems. What are some of the suggestions the resource teacher might make? (i.e., what is the prescription?)
>
> c. What are some possible hindrances toward the complete interpolation of the child's success in the resource room to success in the classroom?

The most frequent answer to Part C was the poor personal relationship between the regular teacher and the resource teacher. For example, the resource teacher is perceived as condescending; the regular teacher is not cooperative; the regular teacher may resent the special status of the resource teacher; the resource teacher resents a regular teacher taking advantage of the situation and making the resource room a "dumping ground."

To prevent such misunderstandings, the administrator should plan for orientation sessions prior to instituting the extra services; roles should be clearly delineated; periodic conferences should be planned; there should be mechanisms provided for the handling of complaints; all details should be planned in advance (e.g., is there a definite procedure for referring a pupil to the resource room or can the classroom teacher, on the spur of the moment, lead a hapless child to the resource room by the scruff of his neck?); duties should be spelled out (e.g., do the volunteer, student-teacher and paraprofessional know exactly what is expected of them?). Cooperation, harmony and coordinated efforts are needed, but they do not occur automatically. It requires hard work.

Tutoring as In-Service Training

The teacher who is in need of "shoring up" can often be helped by receiving guided experiences in teaching one child at a time.

In a very real sense, teaching one child alone can be seen as a sequential step leading to skill in managing and educating groups of children in the classroom. Not too much has been written about the sequential steps necessary to achieve the "behavioral objective" of teaching groups of children successfully. One reason for this is that teaching is often regarded as an art and hence impervious to task analysis. Another is the realization—and frequent lament—that so many uncontrolled variables (e.g., the teacher's personality, the child's personality, the child's background, subconscious fears and motivations, the "mix" of the class, out-of-school forces, covert behavior, etc.) impinge upon the teaching-learning act that it becomes virtually impossible to draw any scientific conclusions from educational research. At any rate, Rivlin (1966, 59) succinctly summed up the need for sequentializing Teacher Education: "Teaching is so complex a skill that careful gradation of learning is as important in a teacher-education program as in an arithmetic class."

There are many administrative means of support which will enable a teacher during a regular classroom lesson to instruct a child individually. In addition to those means mentioned on page 159, the school administrator must help the teacher to consider the tutoring "format" in the classroom. Will the teacher assign independent work to the entire class, and then walk around the room offering the individual attention where it is needed? Brendtro and Stern (1967), in a study dealing with the management and instruction of classes for emotionally disturbed children, consider the merits and disadvantages of this method and suggest a preferred alternative. Among the merits cited are: The teacher can assume a central, dominant role and is in the optimal surveillance position; he can practise "proximity control" (simply walking toward a classroom disturbance can often minimize the problem); he can note "embryonic" behavior problems and is in an advantageous position to deal with them; by moving about from child to child, the teacher develops the feeling that he is exerting his maximum efforts and energies toward helping the child; this moving about furthermore can serve the purpose of reducing teacher anxiety. Some disadvantages of this arrangement cited by the authors are: Wandering in and out of aisles can be distracting to the children; there is a lack of privacy in this tutoring situation in that a neighboring pupil is often interrupted by—and likewise can interrupt—the activities between the teacher and the individual being tutored; the teacher is often tempted to give extra attention to the child who misbehaves, thereby reinforcing undesirable behavior.

The alternate plan suggested by the authors is for the teacher to sit at a desk located along the margin of the room, which can be designated as a "helping corner." Each child, upon completion of his assigned independent work, brings his paper to the teacher. The work is corrected and some planned tutoring ensues. Some advantages of this preferred alternative tutoring format mentioned by the authors are:

1. The tutoring does not interfere with those children working independently nor are they forced to work under close surveillance.
2. The tutoring session is more private.
3. Since the child comes to the teacher (rather than the other way around), he will probably be more willing to accept the help.
4. By sitting at his own desk rather than walking around, the teacher can have ready access to individual pupil folders as they are needed.
5. The motor activity (walking to the teacher's desk and then walking back to his seat) is seen as a reward, reinforcing the *desirable behavior* of task completion. (With the teacher walking around the classroom, the *undesirable behavior* of misconduct and vying with classmates for the teacher's attention had received the reinforcement.)

The administrator who sees tutoring as an essential in-service training process will find means of making the time available to the teacher for this purpose. In addition to the tutoring of individual children in the classroom during the teaching day, there are two other logistical possibilities. The first is to arrange after-school tutoring programs. This has the advantage of insuring privacy, reducing distractibility and eliminating any anxiety or concern which the tutoring-teacher might have about the simultaneous activities of the rest of the class. Also, it could provide additional teaching time for the pupils. A second approach is to establish in-service courses in which actual tutoring is featured in a central role. These courses can be conducted either after school, on weekends or during vacations.

In both these instances the teachers involved may very well be willing to volunteer their time since they will ultimately benefit from this additional training by becoming more proficient teachers. On the other hand, it is not unreasonable to suggest that they be remunerated for their time and effort. Considering the first arrangement, (tutoring after school, on weekends or during vacations), precedent has already been set in that personnel—including paraprofessionals—are compensated for after-school activities. Regarding participation in in-service courses, a similar precedent exists; namely, there are federally funded institutes (e.g., in science, math, special education, etc.) which pay both tuition and stipends to teachers who enroll in them. Credit for course attendance can well be applied in the form of salary step increments. The fact that the in-service training might be conducted by the local school system whereas the institutes are run by the university does not in itself negate the effectiveness of the former. In fact, many universities are beginning to value the experience of public school employees and are including more and more of them on their Education Department faculties. Converselly, many in-service training programs, while sponsored by the local boards of education, often utilize the services of nearby universities.

The ultimate stipulation which the administrator must bear in mind as he establishes various tutoring settings designed to increase teaching proficiency is the provision of guidance and supervision for the teacher-tutor. To be sure, there are some individuals who can benefit to some extent from unsupervised training by virtue of their ability to think introspectively, to evaluate their progress objectively and to interpret reliably the teaching-learning feedback data, thereby correcting their courses of action. The majority of teachers-in-training, however, will never be able to make the same kind or degree of progress by themselves that they could make had appropriate supervision been provided. The supervisor (who can be a principal, assistant principal, public school supervisor, department chairman, master teacher or part-time university consultant) can help the teacher in areas of curriculum, content, methods and materials. He can also guide the teacher in record keeping procedures, lesson planning and evaluations. Long range and short range goals must be established. He can encourage the teacher to think in terms of specific aims, task analysis and behavioral objectives (the translation of which is: What am I trying to teach the child? What are the sequential steps necessary for achieving this? What are the means by which the child can demonstrate that the aim has been fulfilled?). He can show the teacher how to provide for continuity rather than present a series of disjointed experiences. He can point out the importance of tempo changes, regulation of time dosages, variety of activities, provision for some independent work as well as for physical movement during the course of the lesson, routines and organization. He can make the teacher aware of the necessity for establishing proper work habits and study skills. The entire area of attention is a vital one, and there are many techniques designed to reduce distractibility and to increase the child's attention span: however some teachers will not discover these for themselves, but will need professional supervision which can make them proficient in the use of these techniques.

The teacher-tutor must not only become familiar with pedagogic skills and effective in developing work habits, but must also become aware of the child's unique personality and must consider the emotional facet of the "whole child." The supervisor can help the teacher see the child as an individual, emphasizing the need for motivating, personalizing and rendering the lessons (content as well as method) relevant. He can guide the teacher in the importance of making pertinent observations, "reading" children correctly and learning to take cues from them. He can lead the teacher into glimpsing—and understanding—some of the strategies, facades, subterfuges and coping mechanisms employed by the child in dealing with failure experience. He can help the teacher discover means of reversing a negative self-concept and reducing anxiety.

He can conduct the teacher along the path of making individual educational diagnoses and developing appropriate prescriptive experiences. There is a knack (and it can best be learned in the one-to-one setting) in knowing how and when to blend a traditional syllabus with special areas of consideration such as language development (including listening skills) and perceptual training.

Often, inherent in the medical psychological diagnosis (the label, if you will) are hints for amelioration and correction. Hence, it is very likely to the child's advantage for the teacher to know of any significant learning, behavioral or health problem. True, the expectancy studies tend to show that if one gives information to a teacher concerning a child's deficits, the teacher expects the child to fail, thereby making the diagnostic information a self-fulfilling prophecy of failure. What is needed is the realization that there are not merely the two alternatives: (1) Withhold the diagnostic information so that the teacher can consider the child "normal," or (2) Tell the teacher the category (e.g., mentally retarded, brain-injured) thus insuring the child's doom. How about the third possibility of telling the teacher the "label" *plus additional information?* Let the teacher know what the condition signifies, what children similarly diagnosed have achieved, what areas are intact, how compensatory mechanisms (including heightened motivation) work, the importance of extending a good mental hygiene approach to the child, what educational principles and methods might be helpful, etc. In short, provide the teacher with an informal, on-the-spot "mini-nature and needs" course! If handled in this way, the diagnostic information given the teacher need not play the role of albatross—labelling, stigmatizing, defeating. Instead, it serves two very positive purposes. It can make the teacher more tolerant of the child's learning and/or behavioral shortcomings (he saw these anyhow, but now he knows *why*). It can suggest specific remedial avenues (e.g., a child categorized as mentally retarded may need concretization and repetition; a brain-injured child may benefit from structure and a multi-sensory approach; an emotionally disturbed child may require greater flexibility and some permissiveness, etc.).

Perhaps a new set of expectancy studies is needed in which one seeks to determine what happens to learning and/or behaviorally impaired children when their teachers are informed not merely of the "label," but of all the implications deriving from the condition as well. An important aspect of the supervisor's role, then, is to make this information available to the teacher-tutor and to point out the positive specific courses of action which exist but which might otherwise not become apparent had this information been withheld.

In fact, the Special Educators (those concerned with the fate of the disabled) can learn a lesson from the disadvantaged. In many instances, it is impossible to withhold the disadvantaged's "label" (e.g., skin color, speech dialect, aura of poverty, etc.). No one has ever suggested that we refrain from telling a teacher that a child is black or Puerto Rican or Chicano or Indian or just plain poor! This is a matter of fact—and begins and ends in the same breath. What is germane is the consideration of strengths, "hidden positives,"an understanding of the handicapping conditions and the resultant needs. And most of all, what can we do to help?

THE ROLE OF TEACHER-TRAINING INSTITUTIONS

Effecting changes in Education matriculation requirements. The inertia of status quo is a powerful force and must be reckoned with as one attempts to develop teaching excellence. There is no value judgment herein implied; it is quite possible to resist change without adopting a reactionary pose. Education departments create sequences leading to teaching certification, but they do not do this on whim. In fact, there is a built-in system of checks and balances in that State Departments of Education set up the minimum certification requirements and the colleges design courses and course sequences which will enable the student to meet these requirements. The State Departments of Education and the State Universities function cooperatively from the start, participating in mutual planning, advising, and consultations in concert with representatives from local school systems, in an effort to create an end-product which is truly reflective of the community needs. The Education departments do not merely rubber stamp the state's requirements but often superimpose their own upon these. For example, among the certifying requirements set up by a State Department of Education may be a three-point practicum course for any prospective teacher of Special Education. The local college may then say, "Fine. We will set up a practicum course, but in order to be eligible to enroll in it, the student must have taken twelve credits in Special Education."

The point is that these licensing and course sequences, once created, develop, in a sense, autonomy of their own with a certain amount of resistance to change. Again, resistance need not be based upon self-serving motives. Indeed, altruism often plays a role: "We believe that children need quality education. After considerable effort and systematic planning, we have arrived at this particular course sequence. We feel that each course in the sequence has considerable merit. It is a full program—there are no 'free' spots. A change usually means adding a new course and *dropping an existent course.* Now, although we agree with you that the new course being proposed could be extremely helpful to the teacher-in-training, we cannot find a spot for it because all of the existing courses are also helpful. And moreover, they have been proven."

Yet changes do occur. Just about a decade ago, Special Education courses were reserved for Special Education majors. Then, the idea was proposed that regular teachers as well should undergo some training in Special Education. The reasoning behind this point of view was that: (1) the regular teacher may wish to change careers and become a special teacher, (2) in every regular class, there are some exceptional (mentally retarded, brain-injured, emotionally disturbed, physically handicapped, etc.) children who could benefit from the teacher's Special Education training, and (3) since exceptional children absolutely *require* instruction which is systematic, specific, prescriptive (in short, quality education), wheras normal children can often get by (though by no means flourish) without it, the Special Education preparation will redound to the benefit of *all* pupils.

At first this was just an idea. Then parent groups brought pressure to bear (since many of their exceptional children were in regular classrooms or aspired to be there after some Special Education class experience). Professionals began taking renewed interest in this idea, and efforts were extended towards effecting this plan. Today, many colleges offer such courses as "Introduction to Special Education," "Psychology and Education of Exceptional Children," "Special Education in the Regular Classroom," and "The Deviant Child in the Classroom" to students majoring in General Education. Although in many instances, these courses are electives, they are, in other instances, being mandated into the course sequence requirements. Also, whereas at first, they were set up only in graduate schools, they are now with increasing frequency being made available on an undergraduate level as well.

In the opinion of this writer, the inclusion of Special Education training for General Education majors constituted a giant stride towards developing teaching excellence. A second "leap forward" would be for colleges to include for their student-teachers guided one-to-one teaching experiences instead of relying solely upon *group* student-teaching. Although this idea may be readily accepted in theory (after all, the literature is swollen with works dealing with individualization of instruction), there may still be considerable resistance to implementation, based purely on logistics. The paramount question then emerges: *How and when can this "student-tutoring"* (as well as the traditional student-teaching of groups of children) *be arranged?*

Logistical considerations. The prerequisite for implementing change, obviously, is that some genuine commitment be generated towards effecting it. If the commitment is sufficiently strong, then the means will be set forth. Simply stated, "Where there's a will, there's a way!"

One means of achieving tutoring as part of student-teaching*, is simply to siphon off some of the time allotted for the traditional group-teaching experience. This means that instead of spending *X* hours during the senior year in student-teaching of groups of children, *X—Y* hours be spent in this, the *Y* hours being devoted to practice-teaching at the 1-to-1 level. Although this could probably be done, an obvious objection would be that there is no "extra" time in the allotted group practice-teaching time and that any subtraction from it would be tantamount to "watering down" a richly needed experience. This may or may not be the case, and so it would probably be worthwhile to set up such a change (at least on a pilot study basis), observe it in action and submit it to the scrutiny of research.

* Practice-teaching on the undergraduate level is usually referred to as "student-teaching"; when conducted in *graduate* Education courses, it is known as the "practicum." To avoid awkward construction, this book uses both terms interchangeably, except when specifics of time (e.g., "during the senior year") clearly delineate the meaning.

A similar objection would arise if one suggested that it might be possible to create time for student-tutoring by reducing some of the Education courses' content or perhaps even exchanging a given Education course for this new student-tutoring course. The objection may be very well taken. However, one need only recall how Education students perenially complain about "overlap" between different courses in their Education sequence. If, in some instances, this is indeed so, then the extra student-tutoring time might very handily diminish the amount of course content duplication.

Another possibility is to commence student-tutoring earlier. It would probably be best for a half-year to one full year of practice-tutoring to precede—or at least partially coincide with—group practice-teaching. For example, an Education major's Junior year could require the guided tutoring of one child—one hour weekly for the first semester (15 hours of credit), followed by an increase to two or three tutees, one hour each weekly, for the second semester (30 or 45 hours of credit). The actual course credit could be based on a formula such as one point for every 15 tutoring hours.

Methods courses precede student-teaching. It is possible—if the pupil population were made available—to include some guided one-to-one teaching experiences in these courses. At any rate, it is a "natural" combination: a study of instructional methodology plus actual teaching experience.

If the feeling is that no time can legitimately be subtracted from the already existing course sequences, then another approach would be to simply add the time. Perhaps Education majors should get special permission to take the usual sixteen credits per semester *plus* three to six extra hours of credit in guided tutoring. Consider the upper senior year: Full-time is devoted to group student-teaching, meetings, etc. Can't the time be extended so that, in addition to what is customarily done, the student-teacher devotes three hours weekly towards guided tutoring?

Another way of creating extra time is to use time that is not often thought of as college time—Saturdays, even Sundays, vacations, intersessions. At least one such program has already been implemented using this plan. Macalester College (Center for Urban Education, P.C. 006) in St. Paul, Minnesota, devised a program which utilizes the one month period between semesters. Undergraduates acted as teacher aides in designated elementary schools which of course are open during college intersessions. They attended class lectures dealing with methodology, theories and research in "cultural deprivation," and the psychological effects of poverty. They acted as aides in inner city schools but also visited suburban schools for comparison. The participating college staff members conducted the lectures, supervised the aides at the schools (consulting with the teachers), and assigned and graded final papers. Among other duties, the aides were allowed to teach small groups of children. The teachers reported that pupils benefited from the extra attention. As a result of the program, the number of those college students who planned to teach rose from 62% to 70%. More dramatic was the fact that, whereas previously only 10% wanted to teach in inner city schools, now 37.5% did. Among other gains cited were the increased knowledge of the problems and resources of the urban child and community, heightened self-awareness, more precise self-direction, and increased self-confidence.

If extra time is needed—either in the form of inter-sessions, weekends, vacations, or by tacking on additional semester hours to the traditional sixteen per semester—it is not unreasonable to suggest monetary compensation to college personnel and credit and/or remuneration to the students. It may be that special funds—federal or foundation grants—can be made available for this purpose. This is especially true if we are talking about "research," "studies," "projects," "pilot programs," etc. Once the initial experiments, sparked by funding if necessary, prove successful, the practice of including one-to-one teaching as part of student-teaching courses may become Standard Operational Procedure, and hence no longer require special financial impetus.

Sometimes it is possible to save time by allowing the tutees to come to the campus, thus eliminating excessive travel time for teacher-trainees and their supervisors. Some colleges have demonstration schools on or near the campus.

Advantages in initiating student-tutoring earlier. There are some definite advantages in starting the student-tutoring programs early:

1. Of primary importance is that it makes the necessary time available—adding to, not subtracting from, any of the customary student-teaching course elements.

2. It makes it more feasible to discourage individuals who are unsuitable for the teaching profession. Human nature being what it is, it is very likely that a supervisor of student-teachers will be reluctant to "flunk them out" of teaching in their senior year. "After all," she reasons, "they came this far." If the student-teaching is done earlier, it is fairer to both the supervisor—for she must mandate the course changes—and to the student, who can now change majors without excessive loss of time. (In addition, the one-to-one setting is an ideal initial one for the supervisor to observe, attempt to modify, and finally evaluate. It is probably true that if a student is unsuccessful learning how to teach *one* child at a time, he will not be successful with groups.)

3. The converse of this preceding point can be made also. That is, by starting earlier, the student-teacher in need of help can get more help and more time to translate the feedback data into the revised techniques and attitudes necessary for success.

Sources of tutees. It is important to consider the tutee population which will be necessary for this proposed practice-teaching The sources are much more varied than those usually utilized in the traditional group student-teaching. The latter relies almost solely upon public schools, to a lesser extent upon private schools, and still less frequently upon some college-affiliated demonstration school. It is of course possible to draw upon these for tutees for one-to-one teaching experiences. There are, however additional sources:

1. Some universities have established campus-based speech clinics, Education clinics, and reading clinics. The children served by them might very well become the tutees, to the mutual benefit of themselves and the teachers-in-training.

2. Many parent organizations (e.g., Associations for Children with Learning Disabilities, Associatons for Brain-Injured Children, Cerebral Palsy Foundations, Associations for Mentally Retarded Children, Organizations for Emotionally Disturbed Children, etc.) have founded their own buildings and set up their own educational projects (pre-school programs, Saturday and after-school activities, summer day camps, etc.). Some colleges already supply Education majors as volunteers to these programs. The students, in turn, receive partial college course credit. With some planning, it would be possible to include student-tutoring as well in these programs.

3. Parents of children needing special instructional help would hopefully be cooperative in bringing their children to the Education Department's student-tutoring programs, once such programs got under way (planning, publicizing, implementing).

4. A most important tutee source is the college students who, themselves, are in need of tutoring. This group should include the students who voluntarily seek this assistance as well as the under-achieving potential dropouts who are not so inclined but

must, in fact, be identified, counseled, and oriented towards becoming recipients of tutorial assistance. With open enrollment college admission policies expanding, more and more of these students will be available. The tutoring they receive, while serving as compensatory education for *them,* will simultaneously offer one-to-one teaching experience to the student-teacher.

It would probably be a good idea to allow the student-teachers who are planning to become high school teachers to utilize this tutee source, since the remedial subject matter would very often parallel the syllabus of a high school more closely than it would that of an elementary school. Moreover, there is similarity in the ages of high school seniors and college freshman.

All of these sources (the four enumerated ones plus the original three) compositely have two characteristics which hold considerable merit for the teacher-in-training:

1. They are, for the most part, community based. In tutoring them, one can get a direct insight into—rather than only vicarious knowledge of—the community, its population type, its needs and its problems. An important element of such a program then, is the sensitivity training "spin-off."

2. They all have some significant learning problems. This feature is virtually built into the system, since one can assume that if a student had no difficulty in learning, he would not be selected for individual instruction. Teachers can "zoom in" on the most effective educational methods and techniques much more readily when instructing children who need special help than they can teaching "normal" learners. The reason for this is that the non-learning disabled can often learn by themselves, making the most of mediocre or even inferior instruction; hence, the feedback data regarding teaching efficacy is not nearly

as reliable here as when working with the learning disabled. The point of course is that the teacher, while initially practice-teaching with those pupils presenting learning problems, will develop a proficiency that will make him more effective with all pupils, learning disabled as well as normal.

Upgrading the practicum instructor's status. The key person in this student-tutoring program will obviously be the instructor of the student-teaching and practicum courses. Among her many roles are therapist, vocational counselor, mother surrogate to the teacher-in-training, lecturer in the seminars, public relations officer in her contacts with the various cooperating schools, logistics administrator in lining up student-teachers with their practice-teaching settings. The most important role is that of "trouble-shooter" —she must be able to observe a lesson, effectively evaluate it in terms of strengths and weaknesses, and tactfully but specifically offer recommendations to the neophyte teacher in her efforts to shape "teaching behavior." She must herself be a master teacher, able to step in and demonstrate "on-the-spot." She must be highly creative, yet structured. She must be able to analyze simultaneously three variables—the teacher, the learner, and the setting. She must be up-to-date on materials and methods. She must be current in her knowledge of the literature so that she will be able to refer the teacher-in-training to appropriate background sources. She must be energetic, traveling back and forth from the college campus to the various schools.

Clearly, this calls for "top talent". Surprisingly, there is not too much recognition, reward, or encouragement along these lines. And so, most instructors of student-teaching and practicum courses remain "unsung heroes." There are many evidences of this: Rank is usually not forthcoming. A survey would find relatively few full professors engaged as practicum instructors and even fewer among those assigned to the supervision of student-teachers. These instructors devote many more hours to their "load" than do their counterparts who instruct but do not participate in student-teaching, and there is usually no additional compensation for this. Some colleges designate graduate students (doctoral or even masters candidates) instead of seasoned staff members as student-teaching supervisors.

There are several possible explanations for this condition. It may be that the additional time required for seminars, individual conferences and traveling to the various cooperating schools is so unappealing that very few Education instructors aspire to that role. Another explanation is that the aura attached to research and the funding available to it has created a status hierarchy in which high valence is given to research and considerably lower valence is assigned to service (under which the process of supervising student-teaching can be subsumed). It may even be that there is a buffer zone between teacher and teaching that exists in *all* other Education courses, but disappears in student-teaching courses. The former offers vicarious instruction in teaching children, but the latter entails *actual* experiences. One is "in the trenches" in student-teaching, not only the teacher-trainee but the practicum instructor as well. All research and theory fall by the wayside if the practicum teacher cannot herself demonstrate to the teacher-in-training how to manage and instruct children. She must be prepared to "take over the lesson", and must possess sufficient talent to insure success during that lesson.

None of this is irrevocable. If one agrees that the ability to conduct student-teaching courses does indeed call for "top talent", then somehow it will be found and nurtured. One frequently hears the lamentations of educators that "teachers teach as they were taught, not as they were taught to teach." Taken verbatim, this means that teacher-training is literally irrelevant! By recognizing the unparalleled merits of student-teaching with one child at a time, arranging such experiences as early as possible, making these guided and systematic, and upgrading the role and status of the practicum instructor, the teacher-training process may yet become an entirely relevant one!

A MODEL FOR DEVELOPING TEACHING PROFICIENCY

The sum total of educational experiences which a child encounters—and which the school endeavors to provide for him—are so broad in nature, so awesome in scope, and so all-inclusive that they almost defy analysis. It is easier to speak of classroom climate than to choose the first step in a particular task analysis. It is less demanding merely to expose a child to a variety of materials, words, and experiences than to actually impart a knowledge or skill. It seems instinctively correct to be preoccupied with the concept of the "whole child," often at the expense of neglecting to get down to the specifics involved in teaching.

The model on the next page is an attempt to depict the various dimensions of teaching and to consider the many educational vectors (curriculum, objectives, routines, modifications, etc.) in relation to each other. (The word "vector," denoting both magnitude and direction, is well-taken, since the diagram's components depict direction as well as relative importance.)

This model does not contain innovations. The components in the diagram have all been considered, explored, and discussed in most Education courses. The value of the model is not in its novelty, but in its organization, emphasis, and perspective.

Very often, a supervisor of teachers (or the practicum instructor of teacher-trainees) becomes aware that a teacher is not teaching adequately. A general feeling of dissatisfaction is registered and conveyed to the teacher, but this is of little value unless specifics emerge. What is needed is an approach similar to programmed instruction, in which the subject is teaching ability! In this way

Levels for Developing Teaching Proficiency

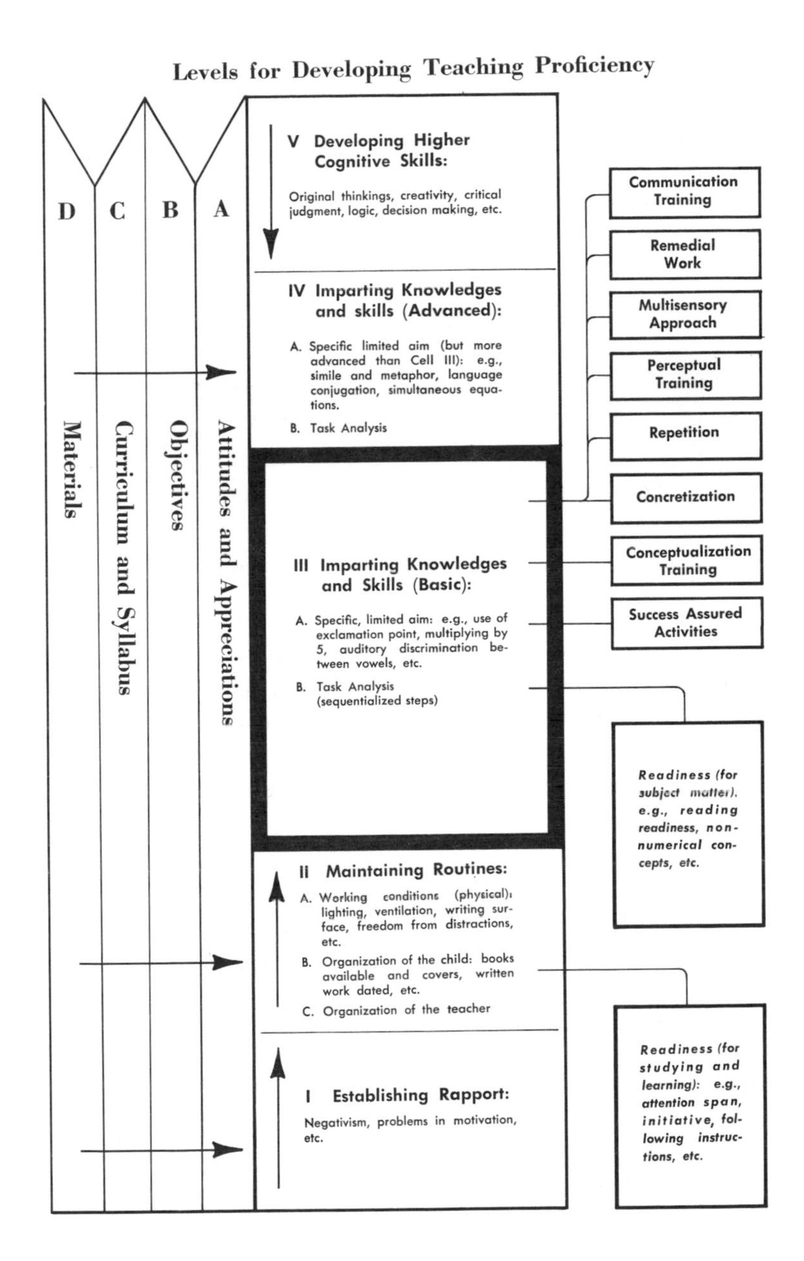

the teacher (or teacher-trainee) can progress from level to level, since the overall skill of teaching has been broken down into sequentialized steps. A consideration of this model, then, can enable supervisors and education instructors to give the teacher precise instructions at critical and well-defined levels of teaching proficiency.

Cell III: Imparting Knowledges and Skills (Basic)

The effective teacher must constantly ask himself two questions: (1) What am I trying to teach this child? and (2) What is the best way to go about doing it? The more specific and limited the aim, the better (e.g., writing the numeral '5,' formation of noun plurals, addition of like fractions, the phonic function of a final 'e,' looking up words in the dictionary). Selecting the appropriate aim is the first step. The teacher must then develop skill in task analysis—understanding the requirements of the task and being able to arrange them in sequentialized steps based upon the hierarchical order of competencies needed to achieve the aim.

This cell, in a large sense, is the keystone to teaching. Its borders have been reinforced to show its relative importance. Teaching, in the definitional concept of the term, means the imparting of a knowledge or a skill. Granted, this definition may seem simplistic and dreadfully incomplete. What about the development of attitudes and appreciations? Isn't the objective of self-realization most important? What about the human element? Isn't equating education with the imparting of knowledge and skills analogous to the archaic notion that the prime purpose of educating individuals is to prepare them to earn a living? Though there is considerable validity in these projected criticisms, one must cut through the morass of tangentials (albeit, important ones) and ask the only valid question: *How can a teacher best help his pupil?* The answer seems obvious: Teach him better!

All too often, a lesson's aim is unclear, or even non-existent. A doctor would not begin surgery without having a specific goal; a lawyer would not start pleading for his client in a directionless manner and lacking a well-organized brief; a builder would not commence construction in the absence of detailed blueprints. It is possible for a teacher, however, to arrange classroom experiences for his pupils without really *teaching* them. "What is the aim of the lesson?" is a totally legitimate question. True, it is pointed and fraught with embarrassment and "touchiness," for in reality we are asking the teacher, "What are you trying to do?" It is surprising how frequently teachers lack a definitive answer to this query, never having fully committed themselves to a genuine consideration of the lesson's purpose—specifically in terms of what they want the child to *learn* as a result of instruction, and what they want him to *do* as a result of learning. An analogy to this question of the teacher's aim is to be found in the current radio talk shows involving a host who conducts telephone discussions with his audience of callers. The most frequent question the host poses to his callers is, "What is your point?" And so, the teacher is asked "What is your point?", in the hope of effecting the emergence of a more clinical teacher, one who deals with children specifically rather than vaguely, goal-oriented rather than purposeless, committed to definitiveness and precision.

There are many qualities of an effective aim. In addition to conciseness, it should possess clarity. It should be stated. The child should be aware of it. It should be obvious to a classroom observer.

The aim must be appropriate for the child, in consonance with his needs. Frequently, children receive visual training, communication programs, phonics lessons and other such entities regardless of whether or not they are proficient in these areas. This is especially true in cases where medical and/or psychological diagnostic information concerning the child has been made available to the teacher. For example, a teacher learns that a child has been classified as having "minimal brain dysfunction." Because many of these children require perceptual training, the teacher *automatically* provides it for him. Due to the large intragroup variability found in this classification of children, there will be some with minimal brain dysfunction who do not require such training. Obviously, the teacher should use his knowledge of the nature and needs of the various categories of exceptionality and the suggested special methodologies as guidelines rather than as absolutes. Teachers, of course, are to be commended for seeking training and becoming familiar with Special Education programs aimed at specific remediation. But *selectivity* is the principle here, for these very programs which can be used so beneficially in some instances can, if employed indiscriminately, become deterrents—*paradoxical* deterrents—to effective education, leading the teacher away from providing those educational experiences genuinely needed by the child.

The "Does The Child Need This?" yardstick should apply to less formal experiences as well. Not only do we want to know whether or not the child needs the Frostig Visual Training Program or the Peabody Language Development Program, but we should be equally concerned with "where the child is at" regarding *any* lesson being taught to him: e.g., adding by two's, writing the numeral eight, use of the glossary, spelling ten new vocabulary words, etc. Does he already know it?

At the other end of the spectrum, the teacher must select aims which are not too difficult for the child to achieve. Finally, such factors as relevancy and pupil interest are also vital here. In short, the teacher's ability to select an appropriate aim is intimately linked with his knowledge of the child.

The teacher's proficiency in sequentializing a task, a highly technical skill in every sense of the word, is probably very much related to the teacher's ability to think introspectively and retrospectively, and then to translate this insight into empathetic thinking. In other words, "How did *I*—or how would *I*—learn this task?" gives way to "How does *one* learn this task?"

Both components, selecting the aim and analyzing the task, are equally essential. By selecting the appropriate aim, the teacher, in effect, shows that he knows *what* to teach; by designing an effective task analysis, he shows that he knows *how* to teach.

There are many techniques whereby the practicum instructor can guide teacher–trainees towards greater competency in these areas. The standard techniques of improving instruction (e.g., demonstration, intervisitation, observation and evaluation, use of a video-tape of the lesson) are entirely appropriate here. Again, the one-to-one teaching setting is an ideal one in which the teacher can learn to "tune in" to the real needs of the child. In this setting, power of observation, in-depth knowledge of children, and feeling for *a child's* development (as opposed to the general topic of "child development" where, in actuality, the teacher considers groups of children, but not the single child) are nurtured. Thus the teacher is provided with the unparalleled opportunity to become expert in designating pertinent aims and valid task analyses—first, for one child, then for a classroom of children.

There are two interrelated reasons which explain why teachers have not emphasized this aspect of teaching: First, most children are able to learn incidentally. They fill in the gaps. They reorder the sequence which has been presented out of order. In other words, they are intelligent, and therefore able to adapt to their educational environment, even in instances of mediocre or inferior instruction.

Secondly, because of our justifiable concern with such elements as classroom climate, development of attitudes and appreciations, and social-psychological factors, the teacher's ability to select an appropriate teaching aim and to perform a valid task analysis—thereby actually imparting specific knowledge or a skill to a child—hasn't been stressed. To many, this has not been obvious, owing to the miraculous ability of normal children to learn tangentially.

Cell I: Establishing Rapport

This cell refers to the relationship which the teacher establishes with the pupil. The teacher must develop skill in dealing with children who harbor negative or hostile attitudes, relating to them in a manner which reduces anxiety and enhances self-esteem. He should see the need for and be skilled in motivating the child. At times, he must resort to non-academic approaches (e.g., a game format, use of humor, reliance on a hobby or interest such as magic, music, art or sports, etc.). Gardner (1969, 145) in recommending the game of checkers as a diagnostic and therapeutic tool in child psychotherapy, believes that "pleasure enhances self-esteem and serves as an antidote to many neurotic problems." It is an axiom of modern educational philosophy that optimal learning occurs if the learner associates enjoyment with the learning experience. A positive "classroom climate," good mental hygiene practices, and motivation converge as the teacher succeeds in making the lesson pleasurable.

The ability to convey to the child in non-verbal communication as well as in actual words that he is accepted and that he can learn is essential. The teacher's confidence in his pupil is often the first step towards the child's emerging self-confidence.

Initially, the one-to-one setting is an ideal one for the practicum teacher to observe the degree of success which the student-teacher achieves as he attempts to establish a positive relationship with his pupil. The one child can be watched closely as he interacts with the teacher. The teacher's performance in relation to the emotional well-being of the single child being taught can be carefully scrutinized and evaluated.

The ability to develop good teacher-pupil relationships is very much related to the teacher's personality. As such, it is most difficult to change. In fact, most supervisors, if given the choice between a teacher who is warm, enthusiastic, and "good with kids," but who doesn't know how to teach, and a teacher who seems to hurt children emotionally, but is adequate in the sheer skill of teaching, would select the former. It may very well be that criticizing one's ability to teach is less personal and therefore less threatening than criticizing one's personality. A great deal of tact is needed. Sometimes, a suggestion of specifics (speak more softly, praise the child more, avoid expressing negative value judgments, try to get the child to relax, etc.) may help. A videotape of the lesson may demonstrate to the teacher that his own tension heightens the anxiety of the child. The whole field of "body language" can be applicable here.

This cell is placed at the bottom of the model, indicating that a positive teacher-pupil relationship is basic to the actual instruction process. Without it, effective teaching cannot occur in may instances. The arrow designates that although rapport is a prerequisite for learning, it does not simply end when formal instruction begins. Instead, it permeates upward and should be a major consideration at all levels of instruction.

Cell II: Maintaining Routines

The establishment of routines fosters effective learning or, to put it differently, disorganization militates against learning. If the child is disorganized, his energies and attention are distracted from the task at hand. Anxiety may be heightened since the child, desiring to conform and to succeed in the teaching-learning relationship, is often held back by an unplanned, non-structured and somewhat chaotic educational environment. Such problems, then, as distractibility, impulsivity, frustration and anxiety are often a function of disorganization. As important as routines are for all children, they are even more so for children presenting learning problems (and therefore very likely to be encountered in most tutoring-training sessions). These children virtually cry out for structure and organization at every turn.

There are three aspects of routines: (1) the physical working conditions, (2) the organization of the child, and (3) the organization of the teacher.

The first category includes such items as lighting, ventilation, proper room temperature, writing surface, appropriate desk and chair, freedom from noise and from excessive interruptions and, in the case of one-to-one instruction, privacy (i.e., parents, siblings and other individuals not involved in the lesson should not be in the same room with the pupil and teacher). In brief, we are concerned with factors relating to the health, comfort and safety of the child, and we endeavor to provide a physical setting which facilitates learning.

The second aspect of routines is the organization of the child. The teacher can best help the pupil by encouraging him to work systematically rather than haphazardly. The child should be taught to prepare for the lesson: appropriate books available and covered, sharpened pencils, previous homework, etc. Uniformity is an important criterion. Since most school children are encouraged to write headings, date their written work, write (rather than memorize) the homework assignment, keep their books in good condition, keep notebooks arranged neatly, etc., the teacher should encourage his pupils (whether in a one-to-one setting or in groups) to do likewise.

Granted, there may be some instances in which more permissiveness is warranted, where any attempt to organize is viewed by the child as tyrannical, where conformity nurtures lethargy. Still, the teacher must be flexible. He must view these as exceptions to the rules—and hopefully temporary. That is, a child may be unable to tolerate structure at first, but through a sequentialized approach, can be guided towards a more systematic work style. In any event, a pupil's need—or expressed need—for permissiveness should never be used as a "cop out" for the teacher who simply has never learned how to teach routines.

The teacher-trainee must learn not to be led by the child or by the situation. He should know what materials and routines are best for the child and for the teaching situation, and endeavor to employ them. If the chair doesn't fit the desk, try to get one that does. If the child can never find the appropriate books, help him with his "storage" problem—often, a discarded carton will do. If the child has too many pages in his looseleaf notebook, tell him to take some out. If there is insufficient light, get a higher wattage bulb. (Don't ask the child if he can see adequately when a 25 watt bulb is used!) The teacher must develop his own standards for organizational behavior and be willing to assert himself and to act on his beliefs. If the teacher (or teacher-trainee) is himself not sure of what is best, he can hardly help the child. Assuming, however, that he does have a good idea of what would be appropriate, he should take steps to achieve the desirable. If a doctor needed clean water for his patient, he would hardly settle for dirty water, just because it was handy! The slogan, *Select, Don't Settle!* is applicable here.

Finally, one must consider the teacher's pattern of self-organization. The topic of planning and preparation is a most important element in teacher-training. To begin with, the act of composing written plans commits the teacher, in a real sense, to some advance thinking regarding the approaching lesson. The success of this lesson in all its ramifications (aim, motivation, procedures, development, methods, materials, summary, etc.) is very much a function of the degree and quality of teacher planning. Education is a serious business and as such it warrants serious thinking, decision making, planning and preparation.

Preparation entails several factors:

1. *Knowing the child.* To truly prepare for the child means literally *to know* the child—his overall level of functioning as well as his specific attainments and needs (e.g., Which letters does he need help in forming? Which consonant blends does he most frequently confuse? Which multiplication facts trouble him?). One must also become familiar with the child's learning style, temperament, profile of strengths and weakness, preferred sense modality, and must select the modifications which will most likely be of benefit to him.

2. *Knowing the task.* In addition to knowing the child and hence being able to select an appropriate aim and make suitable modifications, the teacher must develop a strong feeling for the instructional task. Teaching skill involves the ability to analyze this task and to stipulate the sequential steps.

3. *Employing continuity.* Another dimension to the concept of commitment is the element of continuity. In other words, if the teacher is committed to a given instructional aim, there must necessarily be some continuity between one step and the next one, all of them leading toward the specific, stipulated, *planned* goal. Continuity is fostered in many ways: assigning pertinent homework; parent counseling regarding the integration of out-of-school experiences with the school curriculum; referring to past learnings as well as to future goals during a given lesson, etc. Above all, continuity is nurtured by systematic planning which on the one hand is cognizant of the lesson

development (i.e., the sequential activities within a daily lesson) and at the same time jells a series of these lessons into one or more of the curriculum's broad aims.

There are many variations of lesson plans. Some teachers keep daily plans; others prefer to write them weekly. Some are quite lengthy while others are brief. There are many possible elements which can be contained in a lesson plan. Narrowed down to essentials, a plan should at least designate a clear, definitive aim, list the various materials (including specific pages of workbook and text), and specify the activities implied in the materials (selecting activities which are varied and include some independent work). These activities should be arranged in a logical order. Finally, the plan should provide for some evaluative experience by stipulating precisely *how* the pupil can show whether or not the aim has been realized.

The planning should be a dynamic, ongoing process. The teacher plans *prior* to the lesson. Then, *during* the lesson, he makes additional notes—mental as well as written—concerning the degree of success, modifications to be incorporated into future lessons, items for parent counseling (e.g., drill at home, fostering more mature work habits, arranging integrated experiences).

Homework is an important area of the teacher's planning and preparation. True, there are times when no homework is indicated. In general, however, it is recommended that homework be assigned. This should be planned. The dosages should avoid the extremes of too much or too little. There should be some relationship between the homework and the schoolwork. As with the lesson itself, the homework should also have an aim. Is it drill work? Is it actually a new learning experience? Both, by the way, are valid aims. It depends upon the circumstances and the teacher's professional judgment. The fact is that the effective teacher is aware of the reasons for a given homework assignment and can envision what demands the assignment will make upon the child. In some cases the parent will be utilized as a "helper." In other instances, it is best to avoid this practice. At all times, the teacher should ascertain whether the child understands what is expected of him. This can be done by questioning the child or by letting him begin his assignment in class. The teacher should check the homework and convey to the child that his efforts and accomplishment are recognized, that the assignment is important and that it is neither "busy work" nor punitive. In general, it is best to have the assignment instructions written rather than given orally, dated and kept systematically (say, in a lesson book or in the back of the pupil's notebook) rather than on stray scraps of paper.

Obviously, there is a great deal of flexibility which should go hand in hand with planning. This is necessary to enable the teacher to accommodate the child's mood swings, a sudden burst of creativity, and unplanned but highly relevant current event, etc. However, some critics of the public schools (usually non-educators, often in the fields of politics or journalism), believing that the writing of lesson plans "stifle creativity" and produce stereotyped, dull, irrelevant classroom experiences, take an extreme position and advocate that *no* lesson plans be required. To be sure, master teachers, those highly experienced and successful in various teaching situations, can get by with a minimum of plans. The fact is that their background and expertise contain their plans! Instead of having to write each detail, they have internalized them, and effective teaching is simply a part of them. It is ironic that the same sources which cry, "Down with lesson plans!" are equally vocal in their demand for "accountability." In a sense, the first argument precludes the second. If the teacher is indeed to be held accountable for the child's educational progress, then isn't this very process of keeping written plans (which is essentially a prior expenditure of energies and thoughts committed to maximizing the child's educational experiences) the first step toward attaining this progress?

The planning of lessons, and this includes the assigning and handling of homework, is only part of the teacher's self-organization. There are other important considerations. Is the teacher prepared? Does he know where to sit in relation to the child (at right angles, opposite, near the child, far from him)? If there is only one copy of the text, does the teacher place it in front of the pupil or in front of himself? Is the desk cleared of extraneous books? Does the teacher instruct the child to write even though the desk top is cluttered? Has he provided the proper teaching materials? Is the teacher punctual? Is his record-keeping (plan book, case history data, observation notes, schedule of assignment, various reports) in order?

Very often, the child's disorganization is related to the teacher's disorganization. The practicum teacher, observing that the trainee is disorganized, can offer guidance by enumerating the specifics. The one-to-one setting is ideal for nurturing teacher organization, since it provides for optimal observation and feedback. In addition, there is an obvious sequential advantage: learning to organize one child is easier than—and therefore preparatory to—learning to organize a classroom of children.

This cell has been placed under the "teaching" cells. This means that in some instances the teacher-trainees must concentrate on organization before any real teaching can take place. It often requires time. The practicum teacher must be able to separate the trainee's *teaching* problems from his *organization* problems. By using this model, the practicum instructor can more readily determine the specific level of teaching competency achieved. The trainee may have developed a fair relationship with the pupil (Cell I) but be totally ineffective in actual instruction (Cells III and IV). If, upon closer inspection, it turns out that not only is the trainee ineffective in *teaching,* but that both the child and the teacher are highly disorganized, then Cell II is the area in which the teacher needs immediate help. In the future—often weeks later—when organization has improved, the trainee can be guided towards proficiency in the technology of teaching.

Again, the arrow points upwards. This indicates that the establishment of routines, a prerequisite to actual instruction, is a consideration at all levels of teaching.

Readiness

The model depicts two aspects of readiness—one related to routines and the other to the imparting of knowledge and skills. A child with learning problems may evidence deficits in work habits and in study skills: He may have a short attention span, lack initiative, or be unable to follow instructions readily. The teacher-trainee must be guided in working directly upon these areas. For example, problems in attention may require developing listening skills, reducing extraneous stimuli, keeping unstructured time to a minimum, ascertaining that pertinent visual materials can be seen, employing a variety of materials and methods, keeping teacher's verbalism to a minimum, providing for physical movement, using a game format, and planning classroom experiences which are interesting (Siegel, 1969, 55-63). Tachistoscopic (flash card) experiences are highly recommended, since they involve a "get ready, get set, look" aspect. Similarly, a child who needs help in working independently would require initial small doses of independent work to be increased gradually; also, at first, the level of material should be well within his area of proficiency, to be gradually increased in complexity. At times, the teaching of these skills can be incorporated into the actual subject matter program; at other times, they are literally "readiness" activities—that is, the child must first "learn to learn," then proceed to the regular syllabus.

The other connotation of readiness is used in conjunction with a given subject area. We have all heard of reading readiness programs. These are designed for children who are not yet ready to engage in formal reading. They must be provided with meaningful experiences and intensive work in perceptual and conceptual tasks including language. These broad areas can be broken down into specific skills: differentiating left-right directionality; matching and categorizing various sensory data; discerning likenesses and similarities between objects, pictures and forms. Listening activities and experiences in responding to non-verbal stimuli such as gestures and facial expressions are likewise integral elements of reading readiness programs (New York, 1967-68, 3-7).

Similarly, arithmetic readiness would entail non-numerical concepts such as near-far, today-yesterday, in-on, long-short, big-little, up-down, etc. Penmanship readiness might include a program of arts and crafts, experience in visual-motor activities, and perceptual training.

The concept of readiness—in either connotation—is important not merely philosophically and psychologically, but also pragmatically (in terms of "syllabus"): The novice teacher may well ask "What can I attempt to teach this child who is not ready to learn?" A knowledge of readiness needs and readiness programs may help.

Modifications

These are shown by the boxes stemming from Cell III. At times, the most universally valid teaching sequence will have to be modified to meet the needs of an individual child. In some instances, the diagnostic category will suggest the needed modification. For example, a minimally brain-injured child may require more structure and the use of multi-sensory experiences, a mentally retarded child may need repetition and concretization, an emotionally disturbed child may benefit by some "success-assured" activities and other anxiety-reduction strategies, a culturally disadvantaged child may be helped through additional listening training and a minimizing of teacher verbalism. An educational diagnosis, say, The Illinois Test for Psycholinguistic Abilities' profiles, may illuminate specific deficiencies warranting a particular type of modification. Often, the need for a given modification is apparent: A child who has poor vision may need to sit near the front of the room; if a child doesn't hear well, the teacher must speak slowly and ascertain that the pupil can see the teacher's face as he talks; a pupil who can not grip a regular pencil may require a thicker one; typing may be substituted for writing in the case of some cerebral-palsied; a youngster can be motivated towards creative writing experiences despite his poor penmanship and severe spelling disorder simply by having the teacher become the child's secretary—an extension of the experience chart technique. Frequently, modifications will be dictated by an individual learning style or by a given sense modality preference: In some cases, the strong sense modality will be emphasized; in other situations, the teacher-trainee should be guided towards training the area of weakness—the training sessions interspersing some of the sequential task analysis steps.

The child's very personality is a key consideration. Mallison (1968, 129) advises that the overly concrete child be guided towards using greater imagination, whereas the child who is given to fantasying be pinned down to the concrete level.

Cell IV:
Imparting Knowledges and Skills (Advanced)

Often, when considering the notion of task analysis, one thinks immediately of primary grade elementary school subjects such as those depicted in Cell III. However, it is just as possible—and frequently just as meritorious—to consider sequencing at the secondary level. This is being done much more than is realized. Commercially designed programmed instruction already exists even in college level subjects, some examples being statistics, foreign languages, corrective college English, physics, etc. It is highly possible that the master teacher on a secondary level instinctively teaches via sequencing without necessarily being aware of it. An excellent illustration of this is the case of an experienced teacher of home instruction who was supervised by the author. He has been very successful teaching emotionally disturbed children and is a highly creative teacher. Moreover—and this is important—his concept of himself is that he is creative and flexible rather than structured. He was most surprised when his supervisor pointed out that he is not so unorthodox or unstructured as he supposed. In teaching a culturally disadvantaged child to write poems, he utilized the following sequence without—until it was later pointed out to him—viewing it as a sequence: (1) He introduced the child to Langston Hughes' poetry (they read these aloud using a tape recorder, discussed them, understood and appreciated them); (2) They discussed feelings and the various emotions; (3) The child was asked to list several emotions (fear, rage, etc.); (4) She was encouraged to express her feelings in prose, then in verse; (5) Gradually, the teacher brought in the use of imagery by referring to Hughes' poems (at first, the word "imagery" was not used). A modification was that the teacher did not teach the child formal rules of grammar, punctuation, and usage, but did this functionally—and then, only after the child had gotten the "feel" of writing poetry.

Physical education instructors constitute what is perhaps the single most maligned group of teachers. For years they have been looked on with some disdain, suffering from the "brawn instead of brain" stereotype. The fact is, however, that many of them are superb teachers, largely because they deal almost exclusively in specific aims, observable behavioral objectives and task analysis.

A child needs help in dribbling a basketball? Teach him to bounce the ball (1) while standing in place, (2) while walking, and finally (3) while running. Another child is afraid to catch a ball? Begin by letting him play with a balloon, then a large ball, finally a smaller one; at first, roll the ball down toward him, later bounce it to him and finally throw it to him.

It is essential that the practicum instructor (during pre-service training) or the supervisor (during in-service training) guide the secondary school teacher in becoming aware of the need for and the means of: (1) establishing well-defined, appropriate aims, and (2) translating these aims into effective instructional sequences. Surely, the older child is as equally deserving of quality education as is the elementary school pupil!

Cell V: Developing Higher Cognitive Skills

If teaching in its precise circumscribed sense (Cells III and IV) implies merely the mastery of knowledges and skills, then the development of higher cognitive abilities is situated at the other end of the education spectrum. Higher cognitive skills (including original thinking, creativity, critical judgment, and decision making) are related to how the child will go about learning, thinking, and responding without benefit of the teacher's presence. These skills involve the ultimate in abstracting, enabling one to apply past percepts and concepts to totally unique experiences in a viable fashion, so that maximum meaning may nevertheless be wrested from these new sets of input data. Higher cognitive skills allow the individual to question and examine his environment, his culture, his society, himself.

This cell is placed highest in the model for several reasons: First, cognition follows sensory-motor intelligence. Secondly, original thinking has the prerequisite of previously accepted bodies of knowledge transmitted via education and acculturation. For instance, to consider critically whether or not life exists on other planets demands a knowledge of some basic facts in biology, earth science, astronomy, and arithmetic. Finally, our educational practices seem to follow these chronological steps (arithmetical computation precedes problem solving; activities such as discriminating between fact and opinion often come in grades six or higher rather than in the lower grades; rudiments of music are preparatory to composition courses; the dissertation—wherein one presents and defends his own beliefs and findings—comes at the end of the education road).

Of course the above is an over-simplification and no absolute dichotomy exists. The downward pointing arrow indicates that higher cognitive skills do indeed permeate preceding levels. Torrance (1964, 5) believes that some children learn creatively more effectively than they do by authority, often when engaging in manipulative and exploratory situatons, appearing to be "playing around" —a belief which no teacher, least of all the teacher of younger children, can afford to ignore. Bruner (1970) finds that infants even a few days old are developing cognitive processes rapidly. Seen in this light, teaching is truly a science as well as an art, involving respectively know-how and judgment. The teacher must know how—and when—to transmit skills and knowledges to the child; he must also judge the most propitious moments and means for stimulating original thinking. Again, the one-to-one teaching setting is an ideal initial one for the teacher to develop sensitivity towards the individuality of children and to gain competency in promoting original thinking, creativity, and critical judgment.

Flank A: Attitudes and Appreciations

This segment of the model is concerned with the broad aims of education. These are less specific than the aims included in Cells III and IV. These would not be achieved in one or two lessons, but over a period of time the child could be guided towards their realization. Two kinds of outcomes are considered here—attitudes and appreciations.

Among the attitudes which one strives to create in the child are those which lead to self-esteem blended with respect for others, motivation towards productivity, and sociocentric thinking and behavior. The development of a set of attitudes can create a value system—the converse is also true—based upon moral, ethical, and/or spiritual tenets.

The appreciations include, of course, esthetic interests. They also entail appreciation of others—family, friends, society. Finally, one understands and appreciates natural phenomena—the solar system, balance of nature, the water cycle, the laws of conservation of energy and matter, etc.

In a sense, the attitudes and appreciations which the individual develops lend direction to his education. It is possible for one to be educated and highly polished insofar as the acquiring of skills and knowledges is concerned, and yet lead an unproductive, self-centered, non-goal directed existence, never achieving optimal potential.

The arrows of the flanks point towards the cells, indicating that they impinge upon and influence all levels of instruction. The effective teacher is always aware of broad aims, desired outcomes, objectives of education, and curriculum and syllabus. These considerations lend unification, continuity, and direction to the daily classroom experiences.

Flank B: Objectives

The objectives of education as stated by The Educational Policies Commission (1938) are well-known: self-realization, human relationships, civic responsibility, and economic efficiency. Objectives of education will obviously vary from society to society, reflecting the beliefs and values of a given culture, our objectives being in consonance with democratic philosophies. Indoctrination plays a role in the child's education, aiming at establishing certain beliefs which will stand quite independent of any inherent truth, logical explanation or evidential basis; the other kind of belief, based on evidence and provable sets of rules requires instruction rather than indoctrination. It is interesting that Green (1964-65) in drawing a scheme of a teaching continuum including (in order) conditioning, training, instructing, and indoctrinating, regards instruction—rather than indoctrination—more central to teaching. This viewpoint coincides with the instant model's tenet that Cells III and IV are the keystones to effective teaching.

Just as methodology relates to the *how* of education, curriculum and syllabus to the *what,* the objectives of education determine *why* one is educated.

Flank C: Curriculum and Syllabus

The curriculum has been defined as "the total educational experiences which the child has under the direction of the school" Pounds and Garretson, (1962, 310). Lee and Lee (1940, 165) believe that the child is the starting point from which the curriculum is developed. Our knowledge of the child as a growing, changing, and learning organism and our desire to provide learning experiences for him lead to a curriculum.

There is another way—namely, the converse—of looking at curriculum. True, it is created out of our knowledge of the child and his needs, but once created, it assumes a certain degree of autonomy. It becomes a set of rules, not totally flexible, which does not *reflect* as much as *lead* the child. This can best be seen by the following definition: "A curriculum is a written document which specifies and structures the subject content selected for the education of pupils. It is the basis for teacher planning for individual pupils and groups in local school situations" (New York, 1969-70). An extension of this concept of curriculum, broken down into years or grades, is the basis for the syllabus—the precise scope and range of mastery to be covered in a specific term.

Curriculum—as in the case of objectives—will reflect the given society's mores, culture, and values. The school curriculum of a democracy will differ from those of totalitarian nations. (This stipulation for the development of a curriculum fits in with the previous statement about curriculum, namely, that it is created out of our knowledge of the child and his needs, a major need being to live in harmony with—both contributing to and partaking of—his society's culture, values and beliefs.)

In discussing the meaning of curriculum from any of the foregoing dimensions—planned educational experiences created out of our concept of the child as a growing, changing, and learning organism; educational objectives reflecting the child's society; or a documentation of selected subject content through which the teacher is expected to lead the child—it is clear that the *what* of education is the key consideration of a curriculum. Just as the teacher's ability to select an appropriate lesson aim (Cells III and IV) answered "what is to be taught?" for a relatively short period (a lesson, a day, a week), a knowledge of curriculum and syllabus insures that our daily lesson plans dovetail with the long range goals of education, thereby militating against the likelihood of teaching "splinter skills". Curriculum, then, brings cohesiveness to the aims of the individual lesson.

It is, of course, possible to follow the curriculum in an overly-rigid fashion, virtually ignoring the child's needs, motivation, and level of readiness. In this respect, it can literally stand between the teacher and the learner. For the teacher who is cued totally and invariably by the curriculum but never by the child, the curriculum, instead of facilitating instruction, will serve as a deterrent —and a paradoxical deterrent, at that—to education.

Flank D: Materials

Instructional materials play a vital role in education. They are needed at all grade levels and in all subjects. Materials have a genesis: Educational philosophy translates into methods, which in turn break down into a consideration of materials. That is to say, one first asks, "*Why* teach?" then "*How* to teach?" and finally, "*With what?*".

Education majors usually look forward to "Methods and Materials" courses. These are the "meaty" ones. They often come after some of the more theoretical foundation courses— "Educational Philosophy," "History of Education," "Principles of Education," "The School and the Community," etc.

Montessori paid particular attention to materials: the kinds of materials, the selection of the appropriate ones in sequence, the importance of children learning how to "fetch" their materials and put them away upon completion, the role of materials in fostering independent work habits.

When specific instructional modifications are required based upon a child's individual profile of strengths and weaknesses, the materials necessary to effect the modifications must be considered. Some materials lend themselves to multisensory experiences, others to concretization, still others to drill and repetition; "success-assured" activities, listening training, perceptual training—all entail a consideration of materials. Attention span is lengthened, interest is maintained, and motivation is nourished through proper selection of materials.

The materials can be commercial, teacher-made, or pupil-made. They range from the latest innovations to the traditional (i.e., books and printed materials, charts and graphs, and reference materials). Some subject areas (e.g., science, music, shop, art) justly cry out for materials lest the learning become utterly vicarious.

The availability of materials, an administrative responsibility, often dictates what is taught. For example, a teacher who has planned to teach geography may feel compelled to substitute a different subject simply because a globe and maps are not available!

Recent technology has created an abundance of materials ranging from sophisticated audio-visual aids to programmed instructional workbooks and texts. Moreover, federal funds have made these materials available to an unprecedented degree, setting up regional media centers for cataloging, maintaining, evaluating, storing, and retrieving of instructional materials. And money has been voted by legislatures for the purchasing of them by schools.

As with all "good things," one must avoid surfeit. The questions of *how* to use materials, *when* to use them, and in some instances *if* one should use them, must be asked.

It has already been pointed out (pages 67, 200-201) how too great an emphasis on educational diagnosis can displace our regard for the prescription, how our over concern for the psychological and socio-economic factors can substitute for concentrating on refining our teaching methods, how a preoccupation with the child often makes one neglect to consider the requirements of the task, how innovations, per se, can keep us away from effective teaching, how too rigid an adherence to the curriculum can render us impervious to the real needs of the child.

Yet another deterrent to education, albeit equally cleverly disguised, can very well be the proliferation of teaching materials. Educational materials—innovative as well as traditional, in Special as well as in regular Education, designed for remedial as well as developmental purposes—abound, but do not in themselves insure that actual teaching will take place. Merely reading with the child or exposing the child to reading materials—even the most modern and scientific (e.g., S.R.A., the Sullivan readers, Turner-Livingston series, Barnell-Loft's Study Skills, etc.)—does not necessarily mean that the child is being *taught* a reading skill. Similarly, taking the child on a guided tour, so to speak, of Cuisenaire Rods and Stern and Montessori arithmetic materials is not necessarily *teaching* arithmetic to the child.

Materials, instead of facilitating the child's learning, surprisingly enough can actually militate against it, in that their presence during the lesson can give the teacher the false impression that he is teaching, when in reality he may only be showing materials to the child! To put it differently, the sheer presence of materials gives the teacher *something* to do—if they were not there, since the teacher would not be content to do *nothing,* he might actually begin to teach!

Rawson (1971, 225) tells of a master language therapist who believed that, "If I have some books, paper, pencils, and the alphabet, I can teach a child to read and write, almost always." The author was quick to point out that the therapist "*actually used* a wide variety of materials, but her knowledge of the language she was teaching, her understanding of human functioning, her empathy with children, and her pedagogic skills were *within her*— the result of years of work and growth of personal development and professional maturity . . ."

Probably an excellent teaching aptitude test would be to place a teacher in a room with a child, give the teacher an index card upon which a well-chosen lesson aim has been written, and make sure that the room has no material except two pencils and a few sheets of paper!

* * *

Now that the entire model has been presented, it should be noted that Cell III (imparting knowledge and skills) is regarded as the heart of the model. Reasons for this have already been discussed fully. (See Chapter III—Sequence; Chapter IV, pages 180-184). An additional point that can now be made is that this is the cell—more than all the others—in which the teacher can fall down and not even know it! It is so patently simple for a teacher to delude himself that he is offering the child instruction, when in reality, he may not be at all. ("I am doing something with the child, so why not call it teaching?") The other cells do not lend themselves so readily to this type of deception—subconscious or otherwise: the teacher cannot easily believe that he has established rapport with the child if the child is withdrawn, hostile, and negative. If routines are not maintained and disorganization is rampant, it is not likely that the teacher will claim that his lessons are well-organized. If he does not know the curriculum—perhaps has never seen it—he cannot feel that he is following it. If he has never considered appropriate modifications, he cannot readily tell himself that his lessons are tailor-made for the child.

In a one-to-one setting, the teacher (or teacher-trainee) can be guided in viewing his own teaching proficiency profile based on this model, and can—with guidance, tact, and encouragement—begin to take the necessary steps needed (particularly to strengthen the skills called for in Cells III and IV) to enhance teaching competency.

PERSPECTIVES

If we genuinely desire to get on with the business of educating children, we had better reexamine our past values and notions concerning what is and what is not important. It may very well be that those factors once deemed of primary importance may actually prove to be deterrents to education in that they direct our attentions away from the task at hand—namely to instruct children. The very goals we seek are often thwarted because of two basic reasons. First, they may seem so obvious and unsophisticated that one instinctively recoils from the idea of assigning top priority to them—"everybody knows that, so it can't possibly be the answer." Secondly, the goal, the approach, the element that is needed, is in most cases intertwined with other considerations. Being ever cognizant of the philosophies of the "whole child" and "the whole is greater than the sum of its parts," one is most reluctant to break down a whole. And so the very tree we need may be lost because it is only a subset of the forest!

What is needed is a sense of perspective. This book has steadfastly avoided setting up "either-or" stipulations; it has instead attempted to illuminate those portions of "package deals" which, if separated from the whole (to be sure, only momentarily) might enable one to focus more clearly on the means of promoting teaching excellence. The following perspectives then encapsulate the major thrusts of *TEACHING ONE CHILD*:

- The term "education" almost defies definition. In a real sense, it is seeing, doing, feeling, believing, thinking, imagining, remembering, sensing, guessing, searching, finding, discovering, accepting, rejecting, knowing, questioning, aspiring, communicating, attending, wanting, growing, adapting. It concerns original thought, initiative, attitudes and appreciations as well as mastery of a specific skill via the intervention of instruction. The *heart* of the matter, however, most likely lies in the basic "explaining-catching on" duo of education, and this is the theme that needs emphasis and illumination: The teacher "tells," "shows how," "points out," "explains," *"teaches"* as the child "sees," "grasps," "catches on," *"learns"*.

- In the model, Cell III, and by extension Cell IV, those cells concerned with imparting knowledge and skills, were listed as the keystones to effective teaching, not because the other cells will always pale in comparison. There is a temporal dimension: currently, from the author's supervisory experiences as well as from the observations of many of his colleagues, he concludes that this seems to be the present picture. That is, *within the group of teachers whose overall performance clearly needs "shoring up," many are aware of—and proficient in—some of the other elements depicted in the model but are relatively meager in instructional prowess.* Perhaps with the current focus upon programmed instruction and the knowledge of sequence therein implied, a new model may one day emerge in which Cell III's emphasis diminishes and another cell, say Cell I, (the one dealing with rapport and psychological factors) stands out as the single element which is most deserving of our attention.

- The items mentioned as possible deterrents to teaching are obviously not inherently deterring. Teachers do indeed need to know about educational diagnosis, psychological and socioeconomic factors, innovations, curriculum, materials, etc., but never to the extent that they "nudge out" their concern for instructional expertise.

- Obviously, the child is the ultimate end-product of all of our educational goals. Ironically, though, too great an emphasis upon this ultimate end-product may becloud the immediate issue of helping the teacher develop teaching excellence.

- The key questions—"What am I trying to teach the child?" (i.e., the aim and behavioral objective) and "What steps must I take to do this?" (i.e., the task analysis) are basic. They clearly demand that the emphasis be placed upon the task. Many educational/psychological models do *include* the task as one factor, but it often turns out that the other factors considered by these models siphon some of the teacher's attention away from the task itself. For example:

Prescriptive Teaching (Peter, 1965, 2) involves modifying the variable factors of ". . . the teacher's attitude or approach, his teaching methods, the specific educational objectives for the child, special services, placement and personnel, curriculum, instructional materials, and equipment. . . ."

Diagnostic Teaching (Rosenberg, 1968) includes a knowledge of the task—that is, specific aim, observable behavioral objective and sequence—as well as the ability to recognize and assess the child's "power of the moment" and to be able to modify the curriculum accordingly.

Taxonomic Instruction (R&D News, 1970-71) denotes diagnosing the child's learning style and supplying the teacher with the most effective teaching strategy based upon this diagnosis. This strategy is further based upon the instructional setting, the task, the method of communicating the task to the child, and the medium by which he is expected in turn to respond.

Behavior Modification is essentially a way of changing "behavior" (and "learning" is included under this generic term) by a system of reinforcement. There are really two aspects to this. The first is the task analysis and the setting up of the sequential steps necessary to achieve the particular aim. The second is the reinforcement (i.e., reward at each step). Often, though, one becomes intrigued with the psychological component—that is, the reward in the reinforcement process—and reciprocally de-emphasizes the educational component of instructional task analysis.

- Individualized instruction is the mode of the day. This trend implies humanizing and personalizing instruction. There are many examples and forms of individualizing of instruction. One-to-one instruction is one of them. However, by regarding the latter as merely that—namely, just another way to individualize instruction—one loses sight of the concept of one-to-one instruction as the *epitome* of individualized instruction and fails to see the vast gulf between it and all the other forms.

- Even when tutoring programs have been evaluated, the advantages to the child and not to the teacher have usually been stressed. Where teacher gains are also cited, the teacher referred to is invariably the non-professional (sibling, older child, para-professional, etc.). What is sorely needed is some real emphasis upon what happens to the professional teacher— or teacher-trainee —who practices teaching at the one-to-one level.

- The emphasis of this book is on teachers or potential teachers of *general education* who engage in tutoring during in-service or pre-service training. This does not detract from the obvious relevancy to existing *special education* programs.—e.g., homebound, hospital instruction, "teacher-mom" classes—programs dealing in *only* one-to-one instruction; and classes for brain-injured, emotionally disturbed, mentally retarded, visually or auditorally impaired, and physically handicapped where *some* individual instruction is possible by virtue of the small class size, presence of teacher aides, the use of a "floating" teacher between two classes, etc.

- The principle tenet presented here is that *all* teachers should acquire considerable guided experiences in one-to-one teaching during pre-service or in-service training. This in no way, though, minimizes the value of practice teaching with groups of children as well. It should instead be viewed as a sequential training experience leading up to group instruction.

● ● ● ———— ● ● ●

We are getting close to the answers. One final trap must be avoided, however. It would be a shame if we "blew it" just because we are "getting warm". One must not confuse *proposing* a change with the actual *implementation* of it. Even if the proposing be repeated many times and louder and louder, one must still ask, "But is it happening?" *Diagnostic Teaching* (Rosenberg, 1968, 17) in presenting its order of priorities, states, "... *The assumption has already been made* [emphasis added] that teachers have had the most preparation in the area of curriculum development."

Proceeding on that assumption, the author states that his writing "... *will not* extensively consider how a teacher can develop instructional goals or how the teacher can break the subject matter down into its component parts! [emphasis added]."

What has undoubtedly happened is that more and more universities are indeed instructing Education courses along the lines of aim selection, behavioral objective stipulation, task analysis, and sequence design. This does not mean, though, that implementation is already occurring. Ask any administrator! Does the average teacher have a well defined aim? Does he select observable and pertinent behavioral objectives for the child? Does he sequentialize the task? The answer currently would undoubtedly be a whopping *no*! It takes time and considerable coordination between university Education departments and public school systems to insure that what is being espoused by the former is indeed practiced in the latter.

It would therefore be a grave error to abandon our interest and enthusiasm for "good teaching" (in the definitional connatation of simply imparting knowledge—that is, *"what am I trying to teach the child,"* and *"what steps are needed to achieve this?")* just because we are getting close to it and because it may seem "old hat" rather than innovative.

One is reminded of the adage in which a poor farmer is plowing his field. The soil is pebbly, the terrain unlevel, the plow rusty and dull. He struggles valiantly, doing the best he can under the circumstances. Along comes a young government worker from the Department of Agriculture. He approaches the farmer, points out the inefficiency of his methods, and offers to let him have a government booklet which will provide him with many new ideas about farming.

"Hell," replies the old man, "I ain't farming half as well as I already know how to!"

In the same way, it may be that we are not teaching "half as well as we already know how to."

References

Brendro, L. K. and Stern, Phyllis Rush, "A Modification in the Sequential Tutoring of Emotionally Disturbed Children, "*Exceptional Children*," Vol. 33, No. 8, 1967, pp. 517-521.

Bruner, Jerome, as quoted in Pines, Maya, "Infants are Smarter Than Anybody Thinks," *New York Times Magazine*, Section 6. November 29, 1970.

Center for Urban Education, New York Conspectus No. 006, (n.d.).

Educational Policies Commission, *The Purposes of Education in American Democracy*, Washington, D.C.: National Education Association, 1938.

Gardner, Richard, "The Game of Checkers as a Diagnostic and Therapeutic Tool in Child Psychotherapy, "*Acta Paedopsychiatrica*, 1969, Vol. 36, fascicule 5, pp. 142-152.

Green, Thomas F., "A Topology of the Teaching Concept," in Van Cleve Morris (ed.), *Modern Movements in Educational Philosophy*, New York: Houghton-Mifflin Co., 1969, pp. 232-261.

Lee, J. Murray and Lee, Doris May, *The Child and His Curriculum*, New York: D. Appleton-Crofts, 1940.

Mallison, Ruth, *Education As Therapy*, Seattle, Washington: Special Child Publications, 1968.

New York City Board of Education, *Sequentialized Levels of Reading Skills: Pre-kindergarten-Grade 12*, Curriculum Bulletin, 1967-68 Series, Number 4.

New York City Board of Education, Bureau of Curriculum Development, *Curriculum of the New York City Public Schools*, 1969-70 Series, Number 10.

Peter, Laurence J., *Prescriptive Teaching*, New York: McGraw-Hill, 1965.

Pounds, Ralph L. and Garretson, Robert L., *Principles of Modern Education,* New York: Macmillan, 1962.

R. and D. News, New York: Teachers College, Columbia University, Research and Demonstration Center for the Education of Handicapped Children, Vol. 2, No. 3, Winter, 1970-1971.

Rawson, Margaret B., "Viewpoint: Let's Get Down to the Essentials of Teaching," *Journal of Learning Disabilities,* Vol. 4, No. 4, April, 1971, pp. 224-225.

Rivlin, Harry N., "New Ways of Preparing Teachers for Urban Schools," in Michael D. Usdan and Frederick Bertolaet (eds.), *Teachers for the Disadvantaged,* Chicago: Follett Publishing Co., 1966.

Rosenberg, Marshall B., *Diagnostic Teaching,* Seattle: Special Child Publications, 1968.

Siegel, Ernest, *Special Education in the Regular Classroom,* New York: John Day, 1969.

Torrence, E. Paul, *Guiding Creative Talent,* Englewood Cliffs, N.J.: Prentice-Hall, 1964.

Bibliography

Aranov, Bernard M., "Reaction of Child, Family and Teacher to Handicap in the Child," in Doreen Kronick (ed.), *Learning Disabilities: Its Implication to a Responsible Society,* Chicago: Developmental Learning Materials, 1970.

Ausubel, David P., "A Teaching Strategy for Culturally Deprived Pupils: Cognitive and Motivational Considerations, in Joe L. Frost and Glenn R. Hawkes (eds.), *The Disadvantaged Child,* Boston: Houghton Mifflin Co., 1966, pp. 237-244.

Barratta, Anthony N., *An Evaluation of the District Nine Homework Helper Program, Title I Project,* New York: Fordham University, School of Education, June 26, 1969.

Barry, Hortense, *Teaching the Young Aphasic Child,* Washington: Alexander Graham Bell Association for the Deaf, Inc., 1961.

Barsch, Ray H., "Six Factors in Learning," in Jerome Hellmuth (ed.), *Learning Disorders, Volume 1,* Seattle, Washington: Special Child Publications, Inc., 1965, pp. 329-343.

Black, Millard H., "Characteristics of the Culturally Disadvantaged Child," in Joe L. Frost and Glenn R. Hawkes (eds.), *The Disadvantaged Child,* New York: Houghton Mifflin Co., 1966, pp. 45-50.

Blackman, Leonard, "Research Needs in the Special Education of the Mentally Retarded," *Exceptional Children,* April, 1963, 29, 8, pp. 377-384.

Blackman, Leonard, "The Brave New World of Special Education," New York: Teachers College, Columbia University (n.d.) pp. 1-16.

Bloomfield, Leonard and Barnhart, Clarence L., *Let's Read: A Linguistic Approach,* Detroit: Wayne State University Press, 1961.

Brendro, L. K. and Stern, Phyllis Rush, "A Modification in the Sequential Tutoring of Emotionally Disturbed Children, "*Exceptional Children,* Vol. 33, No. 8, 1967, pp. 517-521.

Bruner, Jerome, as quoted in Pines, Maya, "Infants are Smarter Than Anybody Thinks, " *New York Times Magazine,* Section 6, November 29, 1970.

Center for Urban Education, New York, Conspectus No. 006, (n.d.).

Connor, Frances P., *Education of Homebound or Hospitalized Children,* New York: Bureau of Publications, Teachers College, Columbia University, 1964.

Dawson, Martha E., "A New Look at an Old Idea—Non-Graded Elementary School at Hampton Institute," in *Pioneer Ideas in Education,* Committee on Education and Labor, House of Representatives, 87th Congress, Second Session, Washington, U.S. Gov't Printing Office, 1967, pp. 21-28.

Dewey, John, "Education as a Necessity of Life," in Van Cleve Morris (ed.), *Modern Movements in Educational Philosophy,* Boston: Houghton Mifflin, 1969, pp. 134-142.

Donahue, George T. and Nichtern, Sol, *Teaching the Disturbed Child,* New York: The Free Press, 1965.

Educational Policies Commission, *The Purposes of Education in American Democracy,* Washington, D.C.: National Education Association, 1938.

Fenichel, Carl, *"MAMA or M.A.?, The Teacher-'Mom' Program Evaluated,"* *Journal of Special Education,* Vol. I, No. I, Fall, 1966, pp. 45-51.

Fite, June H., and Schwartz, Louise A., *"Screening Culturally Disadvantaged First Grade Children for Potential Reading Difficulties Due to Constitutional Factors—A Preliminary Report,"* Hunter College Educational Clinic, Hunter College of the City University of New York (n.d., n.p.).

Flowers, Ann M. (pamphlet), *Helping the Child With a Learning Disability: Suggestions for Parents,* Danville, Illinois: The Interstate Printers and Publishers, Inc., 1969.

Frostig, Marianne and Horne, David, *The Frostig Program for the Development of Visual Perception: Teacher's Guide,* Chicago: Follett, 1964.

Gagné, Robert M., *The Conditions of Learning,* Second Edition, New York: Holt, Rinehart and Winston, 1970.

Gallagher, James J., *The Tutoring of Brain-Injured Mentally Retarded Children,* Springfield, Illinois: Charles C. Thomas, 1960.

Gardner, Richard, "The Game of Checkers as a Diagnostic and Therapeutic Tool in Child Psychotherapy," *Acta Paedopsychiatrica,* 1969, Vol. 36, fasicule 5, pp. 142-152.

Gattegno, Caleb, and Hinman, Dorothea, "Words in Color" in John Money (ed.), *The Disabled Reader: Education of the Dyslexic Child,* Baltimore: John Hopkins Press, 1966.

Giddings, Morsley G., "Science for the Disadvantaged," *Teachers College Record,* Vol. 67, No. 6, March, 1966, pp. 435-442.

Gisonti, Frank, *Tactual-Visual Intersensory Integration and Reading Performance of Minimally Brain-Injured and Normal*

Children, unpublished Ed.D Dissertation, New York: Teachers College, Columbia University, 1971.

Glanzrock, Naomi (program director), *Nurse Tutoring Study of the City University of New York: Interim Progress Report,* Grant # NPG-326-01, June 30, 1969.

Goldberg, Ilse, "Tutoring as a Method of Psychotherapy in Schizophrenic Children with Learning Disabilities," *Quarterly Journal of Child Behavior,* Vol. IV, 1952, pp. 273-280.

Gordon, Edmund W., quoted in *The Six-Hour Retarded Child,* a report on a conference on problems of education of children in the inner city, Aug. 10-12, 1969, the President's Committee on Mental Retardation, Office of Education, U.S. Department of Health, Education and Welfare, p. 12.

Gordon, Sol, "The Mythology of Disadvantage," *Grade Teacher,* December, 1968, pp. 70-75.

Green, Thomas F., "A Topology of the Teaching Concept," in Van Cleve Morris (ed.), *Modern Movements in Educational Philosophy,* New York: Houghton-Mifflin Co., 1969, pp. 232-261.

Grotberg, Edith H., *"Neurological Aspects of Learning Disabilities: A Case for the Disadvantaged,"* Journal of Learning Disabilities, Vol. 3, No. 6, June, 1970, 321-327.

Hallahan, David P., "Cognitive Styles: Preschool Implications for the Disadvantaged," *Journal of Learning Disabilities,* Vol. 3, No. 1, Jan. 1970, pp. 4-9.

Havighurst, Robert J., "Who Are the Socially Disadvantaged," in Joe L. Frost and Glenn R. Hawkes (eds.), *The Disadvantaged Child,* Boston: Houghton Mifflin, 1966, pp. 15-23.

Hechinger, Fred M., "Open Schools: They Can Be a Bit Too 'Open' " (newspaper article), in *The New York Times,* September 26, 1971.

Holt, John, *How Children Fail,* New York: Pitman Publishing, 1964.

Holt, John, *How Children Learn,* New York: Pitman Publishing, 1967.

John, Vera P. and Goldstein, Leo S., "The Social Context of Language Acquisition," in Jerome Hellmuth (ed.), *Disadvantaged Child,* Vol. 1, Seattle, Washington: Special Child Publications, Inc., 1967, pp. 455-469.

Jones, Joyce, "Dyslexia: Identification and Remediation in a Public School Setting," *Journal of Learning Disabilities,* Vol. 2, No. 10, Oct. 1969, pp. 533-538.

Journal of Learning Disabilities, Federal News, Vol. 3, No. 9, Sept., 1970, pp. 480-482.

Kappelman, Murray M., et al., "A Study of Learning Disorders Among Disadvantaged Children," *Journal of Learning Disabilities,* Vol. 2, No. 5, May, 1969, pp. 261-268.

Kass, Corinne, in an oral presentation, *Special Education Symposium "Prevention, Remediation, and Integration of Exceptional Children,"* EDPA Project, College of Education, University of Arizona, Tucson, March 7, 1970.

Lee, J. Murray and Lee, Doris May, *The Child and His Curriculum,* New York: D. Appleton-Crofts, 1940.

Lourie, Reginald S., "Experience with Therapy of Psychosomatic Problems in Infants," in Paul H. Hoch and Joseph Zubin (eds.), *Psychopathology of Childhood,* New York: Grune and Stratton, 1955.

Mackler, Bernard and Giddings, Morsley G., "Cultural Deprivation: A Study in Mythology," *Teachers College Record,* Vol. 66, No. 7, April, 1965, pp. 608-613.

Mallison, Ruth, *Education as Therapy,* Seattle, Washington: Special Child Publications, 1968.

Marans, Allen E., and Lourie, Reginald, "Hypothesis Regarding the Effects of Child-Rearing Patterns of the Disadvantaged Child," in Jerome Hellmuth (ed.), *Disadvantaged Child,* Vol. I, Seattle: Special Child Publications, 1967, pp. 17-41.

Meacham, Merle and Wiesen, Allen, *Changing Classroom Behavior,* Scranton, Pa.: International Textbook Co., 1970.

Meidinger, Thomas, "What to Do About It," *Journal of Learning Disabilities:* Letters to the Editor, July, 1970, Vol. 3, No. 7, p. 371.

Morse, William C., "The Crisis Teacher," in Nicholas J. Long, William C. Morse and Ruth G. Newman (eds.), *Conflict in the Classroom,* Belmont, Calif.: Wadsworth, 1966, pp. 251-254.

National Society for the Study of Education, *Forty-ninth Yearbook, Part II,* Chicago: University of Chicago Press, 1950.

New York City Board of Education, *Sequentialized Levels of Reading Skills: Pre-kindergarten-Grade 12,* Curriculum Bulletin, 1967-68 Series, Number 4.

New York City Board of Education, Bureau of Curriculum Development, *Curriculum of the New York City Public Schools,* 1969-70 Series, Number 10.

New York Times, Feb. 3, 1970, p. 46.

New York Times, Feb. 4, 1970, p. 23.

Orlick, Gloria and Ruchlis, Hy, *Guidelines to Classroom Pairing: Reading Tutorial Programs,* New York: Book-Lab, Inc. (n.d.).

Passow, A. Harry, "Are We Shortchanging the Gifted?" in Joseph L. French (ed.), *Educating the Gifted,* New York: Holt, Rinehart and Winston, 1960, pp. 27-34.

Peter, Laurence J., *Precriptive Teaching,* New York: McGraw-Hill, 1965.

Pfeil, Mary Pat, "Everybody's Somebody," *American Education,* Vol. 5, No. 10, Dec., 1969, pp. 21-24.

Pounds, Ralph L. and Garretson, Robert L., *Principles of Modern Education,* New York: Macmillan, 1962.

President's Committee on Mental Retardation, *The Six-Hour Retarded Child,* A report on a conference on problems of education of children in the inner city, August 10-12, 1969, Office of Education, U.S. Dept. of Health, Education, and Welfare.

R. and D. News, New York: Teachers College, Columbia University, Research and Demonstration Center for the Education of Handicapped Children, Vol. 2, No. 3, Winter, 1970-1971.

Rawson, Margaret B., "Viewpoint: Let's Get Down to the Essentials of Teaching," *Journal of Learning Disabilities:* Vol. 4, No. 4, April, 1971, pp. 224-225.

Riessman, Frank, *The Culturally Deprived Child,* New York: Harper & Row, 1962.

Riessman, Frank, "The Overlooked Positives of Disadvantaged Groups," in Joe L. Frost and Glenn R. Hawkes (eds.), *The Disadvantaged Child,* New York: Houghton Mifflin Co., 1966, pp. 51-57.

Rivlin, Harry N., "New Ways of Preparing Teachers for Urban Schools," in Michael D. Usdan and Frederick Bertolaet (eds.), *Teachers for the Disadvantaged,* Chicago: Follett Publishing Co., 1966.

Rogers, Melvin L., "Educational Illusions?" *New York Post:* Letters to the Editor, August 12, 1970, p. 48.

Rosenberg, Marshall B., *Diagnostic Teaching,* Seattle: Special Child Publications, 1968.

Siegel, Ernest, *Special Education in the Regular Classroom,* New York: John Day, 1969.

Silberman, Charles E., *Crisis in the Classroom,* New York: Random House, 1970.

Spalding, R.B. and Spalding, W.T., *The Writing Road to Reading,* New York: Morrow, 1957.

Spicker, Howard H., "Intellectual Development Through Early Childhood Education," *Exceptional Children,* Vol. 37, No. 9, May, 1971, pp. 629-640.

Stern, Catherine and Gould, Toni, *Children Discover Reading,* New York: Random House, 1965.

Streng, Alice, "The Child Who is Hard of Hearing," in James F. Magary and John R. Eichorn (eds.), *The Exceptional Child: A*

Book of Readings, New York: Holt, Rinehart, and Winston, 1962.

Torrence, E. Paul, *Guiding Creative Talent,* Englewood Cliffs, N.J.: Prentice-Hall, 1964.

Treatman, Paul, *Teacher's License Training Text: Assistant-to-Principal, Junior Principal, and Principal,* New York: Arco, 1957.

Van Witsen, Betty, *Perceptual Training Activities Handbook,* New York: Teachers College Press, Teachers College, Columbia University, 1967.

Waleski, Dorothy, "The Physically Handicapped in the Classroom," *NEA Journal,* Vol. 53, No. 9, December, 1964, pp. 12-16.

Worden, Don K., and Snyder, Russel D., "Parental Tutoring in Childhood Dyslexia," *Journal of Learning Disabilities:* Viewpoints, Vol. 2, Number 9, Sept. 1969, p. 482.

Index

DATE DUE

OCT 30 2007			
NOV 27 2007			